D1087799

© THE BAKER & TAYLOR CO.

Individuality and Community

Individuality and Community

The Social and Political Thought
of John Dewey

Alfonso J. Damico

A University of Florida Book

University Presses of Florida
Gainesville / 1978

Library of Congress Cataloging in Publication Data

Damico, Alfonso J., 1942–
  Individuality and community.

  "A University of Florida book."
  Bibliography: p.
  Includes index.
  1. Dewey, John, 1859–1952—Political science.
  2. Political participation. 3. Education—
  Philosophy. I. Title.
  JC251.D48D35   320.5'092'4   78-7335
  ISBN 0-8130-0602-3

The University Presses of Florida is the scholarly
    publishing agency for the State University
                    System of Florida.

TYPOGRAPHY BY COPY GRAFIX
TALLAHASSEE, FLORIDA

PRINTED IN FLORIDA

Acknowledgments

O NE OF THE chief pleasures of publishing this short work is
the opportunity it gives me to express my appreciation and
admiration for two of my former teachers. I was still a grad-
uate student when I first proposed to David Kettler this study
of Dewey's ideas. His encouragement at that time was not surprising. For several years, he had impressed on me the importance of political theory's role in giving men an orientation to
practice. I benefited from his patient but firm insistence that
the study of political ideas requires the most scrupulous accu-
racy and honesty in stating one's own ideas. I value even more
his skillful generosity in showing me how to attempt to meet
such standards. Nor have my debts to him ended. His writings
continue to demonstrate that political theory can be an ally in
the fight against obscurantism and political complacency.

For those of us who were members of David Spitz's sem-
inars, there is a special and immediate understanding of Dewey's
account of a community as a group joined together by the
bonds of communication and a mutual respect for veracity and
responsibility. Wherever he held class—which more often than
not was in his living room—there existed a miniature community. I learned from him that a good argument is not good

v

because there is disagreement but because it makes possible a more secure understanding of political values. My hope is that this work will contribute in some small way to a more careful consideration of the values of liberal democracy. But I am equally glad to know that those values have a most humane and erudite spokesman in David Spitz.

I want to add also a note of appreciation for Professor Manning Dauer, who was my chairman when I first came to the University of Florida. In the early stages of this study, when time was most critical, he thoughtfully arranged my teaching and other assignments so that I would have time free for research.

In dedicating this study to my wife, I do not expect to repay fully her help and importance to me. At a moment when this work left me little time for friends or family, I found a note in my study that simply said, "I understand, Sandra." I, too, understand.

The author is grateful to the following for permission to quote from works by John Dewey published or controlled by them:

Beacon Press: *Reconstruction in Philosophy*, copyright 1948.
Bobbs-Merrill Company: *On Experience, Nature, and Freedom*, edited by Richard J. Bernstein, copyright 1960.
Human Nature and Conduct. The Public and Its Problems. Reprinted with the permission of the Center for Dewey Studies, Southern Illinois University at Carbondale.
The Macmillan Company: *Democracy and Education*, copyright 1916.
Philosophical Library: *Problems of Men*, copyright 1946.
G. P. Putnam's Sons: *Freedom and Culture*, copyright 1939; *Individualism: Old and New*, copyright 1930; *The Quest for Certainty*, copyright 1929.

For Sandra

Contents

Actively to participate in the making of knowledge is the highest prerogative of man and the only warrant of his freedom.

1. Dewey and the Promise of Pragmatism

J OHN DEWEY was a thinker equally at ease with a variety of topics. The sweep of his thought—from a concern with epistemology and ethics to problems of education and politics—reflects the demands that he made of philosophy. Insisting on the unity between ideas and experience and knowing and acting, Dewey's writings range from formal philosophical treatises to occasional columns for such popular journals as *The New Republic*. He would have insisted that these were complementary activities. He believed firmly that philosophy could help "search out and disclose the obstructions" which stand in the way of man's growth and development by focusing "reflection upon needs congruous to present life."[1]

Philosophy, Dewey insisted, is nothing more than common sense sharpened. The philosopher's ideas must be submitted to the same test of practical experience by which men guide their everyday activities. He denied that philosophy has a special claim to knowing truths that transcend man's everyday practice. Theories about a higher reality, immutable principles, and absolute values—all fall victim to the pragmatist's concern

1. Dewey, *Quest for Certainty*, p. 313. Full citations may be found in the Bibliography.

with the consequences of knowledge. This concern was stated clearly by William James: "It is true that a certain shrinkage often seems to occur in our general formulas when we measure their meaning in this prosaic way. They diminish. But the vastness that is merely based on vagueness is a false appearance of importance, and not a vastness worth retaining. . . . the whole function of philosophy ought to be to find out what definite difference it will make to you and me, at definite instances of our life, if this world-formula or that world-formula be the one which is true."[2]

Dewey's view that philosophy must become a form of social criticism is central to understanding the pragmatist's concern with practice, doing, and consequences. It would be a mistake, however, to uncritically equate pragmatism with the practical or the relevant as these terms are commonly used now. As Richard J. Bernstein argues persuasively, there is a "low" and "high" sense of practice and its cognate practical.[3] The low sense of practical is often disdainful of speculation and ideas. The practical man is one who can get things done; he is interested in what works. Students who demand courses which are relevant are impatient with critical, contemplative, and theoretical thought. They want to learn how to grasp, manipulate, and control immediate events. Persons with this common understanding of practice and the practical are likely to misread the pragmatists. While Dewey is concerned with man's ability to control events, his work approximates more closely an understanding of practice in a "high" sense.

To distinguish between the low and high sense of practice, Bernstein reminds us that practice is the English translation of the Greek word *praxis*. *Theoria* and *praxis* are two terms used by Aristotle to distinguish between those activities where knowing is an end in itself and those which have as their purpose an understanding of how to live well. The contrast is not between knowing and doing but between practical science, which through knowledge influences conduct, and theoretical

2. James, "Philosophical Conceptions and Practical Results," in *Collected Essays and Reviews*, pp. 413-14. This essay, first published in 1898, commonly is identified with the beginning of pragmatism as a philosophical movement in America.
3. Bernstein, *Praxis and Action*, pp. ix-xi.

science, which stops at knowledge. *Praxis* also requires theory. To know how to live well demands a reflective and critical understanding of one's purposes and activities. It is this high sense of practice and practical that is closer to Dewey's pre-occupation with acting and doing. "The pragmatic theory of intelligence means that the function of mind is to project new and more complex ends—to free experience from routine and from caprice. Not the use of thought to accomplish purposes already given either in the mechanism of the body or in that of the existent state of society, but the use of intelligence to liberate and liberalize action, is the pragmatic lesson. . . . To elaborate these convictions of the connection of intelligence with what men undergo because of their *doings* and with the emergence and direction of the creative, the novel, in the world is of itself a program which will keep philosophers busy until something more worthwhile is forced upon them."[4]

Dewey's social and political thought also is likely to be misunderstood without some knowledge of its philosophical underpinnings. Dewey himself insisted that his theory of politics, and especially of democracy, developed out of his philosophy.[5] For example, his emphasis on the need for communication in a democracy is a point better understood in light of his more philosophical argument that only through a community of investigators can we know reality rationally.

Because Dewey has said so much about scientific method, inquiry, and practice, his interpreters often have ignored his views about the purposes or ends of man's activities. Louis

---

4. Dewey, *On Experience, Nature, and Freedom*, pp. 65-67, emphasis added.

5. In an address delivered in 1918, Dewey writes that "there has been, roughly speaking, a coincidence in the development of modern experimental science and of democracy. Philosophy has no more important question than a consideration of how far this may be mere coincidence, and how far it marks a genuine correspondence. Is democracy a comparatively superficial human expedient, a device of petty manipulation, or does nature itself, as that is uncovered and understood by our best contemporaneous knowledge, sustain and support our democratic hopes and aspirations? Or, if we choose to begin arbitrarily at the other end, if to construct democratic institutions is our aim, how then shall we construe and interpret the natural environment and natural history of humanity in order to get an intellectual warrant for our endeavors, a reasonable persuasion that our undertaking is not contradicted by what science authorizes us to say about the structure of the world?" "Philosophy and Democracy," in *Characters and Events*, 2:849.

Hartz's *The Liberal Tradition in America* reflects this neglect and the tendency to equate pragmatism with the practical in a low sense. Americans, he argues, take for granted the Lockean image of an atomistic society which values the pursuit of self-interest. Rather than engaging in public debate over the ends of politics, he asserts that Americans are only interested in refining the techniques for making the system work. This attitude, he concludes, represents the political triumph of pragmatism in America (pp. 204-5, 264, 271). I do not disagree with Hartz's central thesis that much of American political thought rests on a series of unexamined Lockean values, but with his contention that Dewey's thought fits neatly into this scheme. Some of Dewey's writings justify Hartz's interpretation, but a great deal does not. Insofar as this is true, Hartz's account of liberalism in America can stand some partial revision.

In the more recent *The Political Theory of John Dewey*, A. H. Somjee offers a fairly novel and interesting interpretation of Dewey's political writings. Focusing on Dewey's theory of knowledge, Somjee presents Dewey's political writings as largely an effort to develop empirical concepts for political investigation. Somjee's thesis is convincing. Much of Dewey's thought is indeed preoccupied with issues of empirical inquiry. Dewey's confidence in the power of knowledge and reason to manipulate social forces systematically and "scientifically" is rooted in his transfer of a model of physical inquiry directly to the problem of controlling social forces. However, Somjee goes too far when he argues that the core of Dewey's political thought is an effort to develop a "conceptual framework for the investigation of political phenomena" (see esp. pp. xi-xii, 178). What is missing from Somjee's discussion is some analysis of Dewey's substantive ideas about certain traditional problems of politics. For instance, it will be shown that Dewey was more concerned with clarifying and advocating the participation of the public in a democracy than he was with developing empirical concepts for investigating the nature of the public. And his theory of liberalism, for example, is not a scientific model for studying politics—it is a new analysis of political life.

The most frequent criticism of Dewey's ethics, educational theory, and political theory is that he develops a method for solving problems at the expense of any theory or vision of the ends or purposes of men's activities.[6] This criticism is exaggerated. Dewey's writings do provide a basis for distinguishing among experiences which are valuable and those which are not.[7] Pragmatism as a philosophy of experience and method is the thread that runs through Dewey's work, but the thread is knotted securely in individuality and community. This is most evident in his ethical theory: Only social ends are reasonable, he argues, since they enhance the individual's life by developing and enriching his relationships with others. I believe Dewey's political theory makes essentially the same case. He objects to any explanation of political issues in terms of opposition between the individual and the social and between authority and freedom. He believes that such analyses distort the true nature of experience. The individual and the collective are not in opposition; rather, he says, they are different parts of an experience that finds its fulfillment in community life. The good community is one where men are aware of their common interests in the progressive growth of each individual.

In Dewey's theory that democracy is a way of life, politics and community are inseparable. Successful democracy depends on the existence of a community, the people organized as a "public." Politics is viewed as an activity for solving men's collective problems through group participation and action. But individuals must learn how to be citizens, how to cooperate actively with others who share their desire to better understand some problem. This is clearly evident in Dewey's writings on education: He wanted the student to participate actively in the discovery of knowledge, not to be a passive recipient of authoritative teachings. He maintained that only through open inquiry and communication can citizens in a democracy learn that the state is more than just a machine for insuring personal safety and common convenience. Democracy encourages an

6. This common objection to these different aspects of Dewey's thought can be found in Cohen, *Studies in Philosophy and Science*, pp. 139–75; Hofstadter, *Anti-Intellectualism*, esp. pp. 372–77; Bourne, *War and the Intellectuals*, pp. 53–64.
7. Although I believe that Dewey's educational writings are least successful in accomplishing this, his theory of education has been defended by Hullfish in *Toward a Democratic Education*, pp. 99–118.

awareness of shared values and the development of common loyalties that are the marks of a community. At a time when many people are puzzling again the meaning of democracy[8]— what it demands of a citizen, how it affects the quality of his life—there is sufficient reason for becoming re-acquainted with Dewey's social and political ideas.

8. Particularly valuable in dealing with these themes are Bachrach, *Theory of Democratic Elitism*; Pranger, *Eclipse of Citizenship*; Keynes and Ricci, eds., *Political Power, Community and Democracy*. The readings collected by Minar and Greer in *Concept of Community* are helpful for understanding how the problems of community enter into a theory of politics.

2. Pragmatist Foundations
Instrumentalism and Naturalism

IN DEWEY'S WORK, there is a logical, as well as chronological, progression in his thought from a consideration of topics in philosophy, especially epistemology and ethics, to the subjects of education and politics. There is little sense in arguing this connection now; the point is that many of the statements in Dewey's later writings often carry a meaning that is informed and circumscribed by the positions argued in the earlier works.

THE MEANING OF INSTRUMENTALISM

By focusing on the nature of the activity which bridges ideas and experiences, Dewey's theory of inquiry or instrumentalism is significant for four major reasons: the emphasis on the practical effects of thought, the focus on specific situations, the account of the problematic in experience as an existential situation, and the location of rationality in the activity of inquiry and communication. In his later writings, these themes reappear in his theory of politics as an art for solving specific social problems, in his confidence in intelligence or "scientific method" as a technique for resolving social conflict, and in his argument that formation of the democratic "public" is critical to

7

the success of democracy. Instrumentalism unites these various philosophical and political considerations by inquiring into the nature and meaning of *practice*, the activity which combines means and ends, ideas and experience. This emphasis distinguishes Dewey's pragmatism from that of either Charles Peirce or William James.[1] Peirce is interested mainly in the structure of ideas; James is more concerned with the particular actions which result from believing an idea. Dewey mediates between these two concerns by focusing on the nature of the activity that links ideas and experience.

All pragmatists insist that there is a vital connection between knowing and acting. This insistence originated in Peirce's 1877 essay "How to Make Our Ideas Clear." Briefly, Peirce's analysis of the logic of science was guided by his desire to supply a method for arbitrating among conflicting meanings given a concept or abstract statement. He is especially critical of scholasticism for substituting increasingly abstract concepts for the concept which needs to be explained. The scholastic method, he complains, will offer you a definition of "canary" by distinguishing canaries from other "birds" which, in turn, have to be distinguished from other "vertebrates." Scholasticism builds a spiraling staircase which leads us into an increasingly abstract realm of meaning. "Rising through *birds, vertebrates, animals, living creatures, natural objects, things,* we come, in the ninth remove from *canary-birds,* to *substances . . .* " (Peirce's emphasis).[2]

In contrast to scholasticism, Peirce offers a "prescription" for translating an abstract concept into an operational form which makes a common understanding possible because of a similar set of experiences. His major maneuver is to transfer the problem of disputed meaning from the cognitive realm to the realm of experience; more exactly, he identifies the meaning of a concept with the total possible experiences of that concept (5.403, 5.402, 5.438). His best-known example is a description of how to make clear the meaning of the concept "lithium":

1. For a systematic comparison of Peirce, James, and Dewey, see Moore, *American Pragmatism.* A short but incisive comparison is made also by White, *Science and Sentiment,* chaps. 7, 8, 11.

2. Peirce, *Collected Papers,* volume 5, paragraphs 388–410, 500, hereafter cited as 5.388–410, 5.500.

"If you look into a textbook of chemistry for a definition of *lithium*, you may be told that it is that element whose atomic weight is 7 very nearly. But if the author has a more logical mind he will tell you that if you search among minerals that are vitreous, translucent, grey or white, very hard, brittle, and insoluble, for one which imparts a crimson tinge to an unluminous flame, this mineral being triturated with lime or witherite rats-bane, and then fused, can be partly dissolved in muriatic acid; and if this solution be evaporated, and the residue be extracted with sulphuric acid, and duly purified, it can be converted by ordinary methods into a chloride, which being obtained in the solid state, fused and electrolyzed with half a dozen powerful cells, will yield a globule of a pinkish silvery metal that will float on gasoline; and the material of *that* is a specimen of lithium. The peculiarity of this definition—or rather the precept that is more serviceable than a definition—is that it tells you what the word lithium denotes by prescribing what you are to *do* in order to gain a perceptual acquaintance with the object of the word" (2.330, Peirce's emphasis).

If you do X, then you will experience Y. This is Peirce's prescription for determining the meaning of a concept, a prescription which he gives the name pragmatism. Given Peirce's example and even this adumbrated version of his account of meaning, it becomes easier to understand why pragmatists insist that a "practical consideration" is an important feature of a concept's meaning. A practical consideration is not something useful in some materialistic sense; rather, it points to the link between a particular line of conduct and the experiences it entails. A practical consideration, Peirce explains, is similar to a logical consequence. "In the language of logic 'consequence' does not mean that which follows, which is called the *consequent*, but means the fact that a consequent follows from the antecedent" (4.435n1, Peirce's emphasis). A logical consequence is neither the antecedent nor the conclusion but the relationship between them. Similarly, those perceptions accompanying the performance of some operation are a practical consideration; nothing is said about the crassly utilitarian nature of the outcome.

This side of Peirce's thought is very close to positivism. It equates the meaning of a concept with the verification process used to test the possible experiences the concept suggests. The pragmatic prescription translates such statements as "This is hard" into the form "If you attempt to scratch the object, you will not succeed." The only way to determine the difference between the meaning of "This is hard" and "This is soft" is to engage in a particular type of action. Apart from the consequences implied in the meaning of such concepts, the concepts are quite literally meaningless. Reason is neither pure cognition nor pure practice. Understanding and knowledge result when the conceivable effects of some concept are combined with the actions suggested by the cognitive antecedent. Peirce concludes that "the elements of every concept enter into logical thought at the gate of perception and make their exit at the gate of purposive action; and whatever cannot show its passports at both these two gates is to be arrested as unauthorized by reason" (5.212).

While Peirce's theory of meaning was part of his response to such larger issues as the controversy between metaphysical realists and nominalists, one additional comment here will satisfy our desire to anticipate certain pragmatist themes central to Dewey's thought. What is appealing about scientific method in general, and Peirce's pragmatic prescription in particular, is its promise to substitute accredited belief for doubt and thereby provide men with an orientation to practice. As long as men widely disagree about which opinions are true, Peirce argues, doubt is inevitable. What is needed is some guiding principle which makes agreement, and thus belief, possible. Science answers this need. The public feature of scientific inquiry justifies confidence that our belief is universal rather than particular, objective rather than subjective. Peirce's own confidence is reflected in his judgment that "different minds may set out with the most antagonistic views, but the progress of investigation carries them by a force outside of themselves to one and the same conclusion" (5.407, 5.358).

The social principle implicit in knowing the world is captured by the phrase "the community of investigators." Men form a community because of the way inquiry is conducted; the association is characterized by certain common understandings. Community, as Dewey will argue at length, is a function of communication. Thus, Peirce anticipates Dewey's location of rationality; i.e., the certification of beliefs and values as true or good, within the activity of ideal communication and inquiry.

While Dewey shares Peirce's interest in the logic of science, he is much more inclined to tie that interest to his comments on the status of social and political philosophy. He expands the pragmatic account of the methodological characteristics of science into an attack on abstract and formal theories of ethics and politics. In such works as *Reconstruction in Philosophy* and *The Quest for Certainty*, Dewey is especially critical of idealist philosophers for misunderstanding the nature of knowledge. He argues that they err in assuming that the object of knowledge is some "antecedent reality" of constitutive thought or a priori forms which reflective reason is supposed to be able to grasp. Furthermore, they misidentify the rational and the real. "What is known, what is true for cognition, is what is real in being" (*Quest for Certainty*, p. 21). This higher reality is then endowed with those values which express the best in man. Since the reality known by pure reason is considered unchanging, philosophical principles are also viewed as eternal and universal. Quite simply, Dewey's first complaint is that all this lacks any foundation in light of the pragmatic account of meaning.

Dewey's complaint is not reducible to the positivist objection that idealism is nonempirical. He is equally critical of that extreme empiricism which mistakenly reduces all experience to isolated and unique sensory perceptions. This "sensational empiricism" shares the idealist belief that all reflective knowledge must be referred back to something already known. For the idealists, this antecedent reality is an a priori system; for the empiricists, it is a set of previous sensations. "The quarrel between them is strictly domestic, all in the family" (*Quest for Certainty*, p. 182).

Neither the idealists nor the empiricists, Dewey continues, understand the place of reason *in* experience. Ideas must be understood in terms of the activity which attends any problem solving, whether it be intellectual puzzles or practical dilemmas. Succinctly stated, the core doctrine of Dewey's instrumentalism is that "all deliberation is a search for a *way* to act."[3]

3. Dewey, *Human Nature and Conduct*, p. 182; *Essays in Experimental Logic*, pp. 16, 245, Dewey's emphasis.

Instead of seeing ideas as something that reason brings to experience, Dewey asserts that they develop out of experience. To understand Dewey on this point, it is necessary to note that he locates the knowing activity within a problematic experience. Much of the time, men act simply on the basis of habit or else with that automatic certainty based on previous knowledge. For example, the skilled worker operates his machine without pausing to examine his activity. But at other times, some disturbance in the interaction between a man and his environment interrupts this pattern. Such conflicts, disturbances, and difficulties are stimuli to thought: An idea emerges as a proposal for acting in order to deliberately reorganize the experience and transform a problematic situation into a settled one. Knowing, then, is a type of activity intermediate in the development of an experience. Inquiry begins because something has gone wrong; it ends when the problem has been remedied. Dewey elaborates: "Let us then by way of experiment, follow this suggestion. Let us assume that among real objects in their values and significances, real oppositions and incompatibilities exist; that these conflicts are both troublesome in themselves, and the source of all manner of further difficulties—so much so that they may be suspected of being the source of all man's woe, of all encroachment upon and destruction of value, of good. Suppose that thinking is, not accidentally, but essentially, a way, and the only way that proves adequate of dealing with these predicaments—that being 'in a hole,' in difficulty, is the fundamental 'predicament' of intelligence. Suppose when effort is made in a brute way to remove these oppositions and to secure an arrangement of things which means satisfaction, fulfillment, happiness, that the method of brute attack, of trying directly to force warrings into peace fails; suppose then an effort to effect the transformation by an indirect method—by inquiry into the disordered state of affairs and by framing views, conceptions, of what the situation would be like were it reduced to harmonious order. Finally, suppose that upon this basis a plan of action is worked out, and that this plan, when carried into overt effect, succeeds infinitely better than the brute method of attack in bringing about the desired consummation. Suppose again this indirection of activity is precisely what we mean by thinking. Would it not hold that harmony is the end and the test of thinking? that observations are pertinent and ideas correct just so far as, overtly acted upon, they succeed in removing the undesirable, the inconsistent."[4]

The foregoing passage introduces all the key elements in Dewey's theory of inquiry. Aside from the emphasis on action and on the social and biological context within which knowing is said to occur, the statement also suggests the experimental quality of our ideas and acts. Since ideas must be tested by being tried, perception and conception progress side by side. Theory and practice work together to transform an indeterminate situation into a determinate one. This argument is Dewey's answer to the traditional epistemological distinction between subject and object, the knower and the known. In their book *Knowing and the Known*, Dewey and Arthur Bentley argue that knowing and the known are "twin aspects of a common fact," some interaction between organism and environment (p. 53). Stripped of its technical language, Dewey's argument is that experience is both direct and objective, but to experience something is not to know it. Knowing involves a time sequence; that which is known is the conclusion of reflective inquiry as it reorganizes experience.

Inquiry does not make experience more real, says Dewey; rather, it makes it more controllable. "Experience of that phase of objects which is constituted by their relations, their interactions, with one another, makes possible a new way of dealing with them, and thus eventually creates a new kind of experienced objects, not more real than those which preceded but more significant, and less overwhelming and oppressive." What is altered by inquiry is *our* relationship to some object or experience. At times, Dewey seems to be saying that this is the only change which occurs. For example, "in astronomy . . . we cannot introduce variation into remote heavenly bodies. But we can deliberately alter the conditions under which we observe them, which is the same thing" (*Quest for Certainty*, pp. 84, 219-20). But he also says that the experience itself changes: reflective inquiry produces a reconstructed experience different from the antecedent experience. It is this side of Dewey's theory of inquiry which entails an activist and reform-oriented style of politics.

4. Dewey, *Influence of Darwin*, pp. 132-33.

Dewey opposed pragmatism to both idealism's "spectator" theory of knowledge and extreme empiricism's "retrospective" theory of knowledge. Throughout his writings, he hammers the points that experience is the result of interaction between organism and environment and that knowledge, therefore, is the result of some activity. His observations on the history of ideas further bring out the social and practical implications of his quarrel with those philosophies which set up a series of dualisms between ideas and experience, knowing and acting. Dewey argues that ideas should be examined in the specific historical situations in which they arise. His purpose is partly to make us more skeptical of previous philosophies by dating them: The notion that they represent final truths becomes inappropriate when we see them as responses to particular circumstances. Whenever we become self-conscious about the activity of philosophy, he argues, it is evident that the "problems and subject matter of philosophy grow out of stresses and strains in the community life in which a given form of philosophy arises." He maintains that even the most abstract and metaphysical systems of thought are tied to very practical concerns, particularly where men need to cope with uncertainty in their affairs.

Nature, Dewey reminds us, is a mixture of the certain and the uncertain, stability and change, indeterminance and probability. Uncertainty is a universal quality of human experience. Consequently, action or practice always involves risks: Things may not turn out as expected. But men find it difficult to live with such uncertainty. "The quest for certainty is a quest for a peace which is assured, an object which is unqualified by risk and the shadow of fear which actions cast. For it is not uncertainty *per se* which men dislike, but the fact that uncertainty involves us in peril of evils." Men have sought to escape these perils through a variety of means. Prior to philosophy, they resorted to religious rites in an attempt to propitiate those powers believed responsible for the intrusion of the unexpected or the accidental. This distinction between the ordinary and the extraordinary marked the first great division in thought.[5]

5. Dewey, *Reconstruction*, p. v; *Quest for Certainty*, pp. 8, 10–11. Much of Dewey's account of the first quests for certainty is supported by the discussion of mythopoeic thought in Frankfort et al., *Before Philosophy*.

Greek thought introduced another major division in man's beliefs about the world: the invidious distinction between experience and a higher reality known only to cognition. This distinction was also a response to man's quest for certainty. Given the then prevailing view that experience never rises above the "level of the particular, the contingent, and the probable," Greek philosophers believed that the justification of beliefs about the virtuous life could not be rooted in experience alone. Metaphysics solved the dilemma. Reason, it was claimed, can discover principles that transcend experience. Consequently, the "verdict of our most enduring philosophic tradition" has been that "quest for complete certainty can be fulfilled in pure knowing alone." Philosophy, like religion, became separated from man's ordinary conditions and circumstances. Sidney Hook summarizes Dewey's treatment of historical philosophies: "Just as there is a method behind madness so there is a meaning behind nonsense. Dewey's hypothesis is that even in a crazy patchwork quilt of metaphysics, particularly if it wins acceptance, we can find some response to the same difficulties and predicaments of life which are at the basis of political, cultural, and social struggles."[6]

However, Dewey's approach to the history of ideas has a positive side: Ideas are an important guide to practice. "When it is acknowledged that under disguise of dealing with ultimate reality, philosophy has been occupied with the precious values embedded in social traditions, that it has sprung from a clash of social ends and from a conflict of inherited institutions with incompatible contemporary tendencies, it will be seen that the task of future philosophy is to clarify men's ideas as to the social and moral strifes of their own day" (Reconstruction, p. 26).

The consequences of separating philosophy from experience have become especially acute in the modern age. The rise of natural science has been accompanied by an increased number and diversity of secular interests and values. Consequently, philosophical systems seem even more remote from the affairs of most men. Philosophical conceptions about a higher reality and fixed moral ends provide no real guidance for securing goods and values in experience. They provide no solid founda-

6. Dewey, Quest for Certainty, p. 8; Hook, John Dewey, p. 44.

tion for men's beliefs about ends to be sought, goods to be desired, and evils to be averted. Where traditional conceptions of values hold sway, philosophy simply accentuates the crisis. What has happened is that men follow one mental pattern in their practical activities and another in thinking about values. "We are pulled in opposite directions. We have not as yet a philosophy that is modern in other than a chronological sense." The most important problem of the modern age, says Dewey, is resolving the interaction among beliefs which "scientific inquiry vouchsafes, beliefs about the actual structure and processes of things," and beliefs about the values which should guide conduct.[7] Means and ends need to be connected; theory needs to be united with practice.

In the natural sciences, Dewey believes that ideas and experience have been brought together. Therefore, physical inquiry becomes his model for all inquiry. What attracts Dewey to physical inquiry is science's emphasis on doing. Knowing in the sciences is a "certain kind of intelligently conducted doing; it ceases to be contemplative and becomes in a true sense practical." The best promise for philosophy, therefore, is also to become operative and "experimental." Philosophical reconstruction that brings ideas and experience together would "relieve men of having to choose between an impoverished and truncated experience on one hand and an artificial and impotent reason on the other" (*Reconstruction*, pp. 101, 121).

Dewey's program of reconstruction has both its negative and positive aspects. Negatively, it leads him to enter the following criticism of other social and political theories: "We plunge into the heart of the matter, by asserting that these various theories suffer from a common defect. They are all committed to the logic of general notions under which specific situations are to be brought. . . . The discussion goes on in terms of *the* state, *the* individual; the nature of institutions as such, society in general" (Dewey's emphasis). Aside from being abstract and formal, Dewey also criticizes such theories for blocking the inquiry and experimentation necessary for successful practice. "They are general answers supposed to have a universal meaning that covers and dominates all particulars. Hence they do not assist

7. Dewey, "Challenge to Liberal Thought," in *Problems of Men*, pp. 154–55; *Quest for Certainty*, pp. 26–48.

inquiry. They close it. They are not instrumentalities to be employed and tested in clarifying concrete social difficulties. They are ready-made principles to be imposed upon particulars in order to determine their nature" (*Reconstruction*, pp. 188, 189).

According to Dewey, progress in the natural sciences "has consisted precisely in the invention of an equipment" for distinguishing the true from the false "by specific modes of treatment in specific situations." In modeling his instrumentalism after the pattern of inquiry characteristic of natural or physical science, Dewey seems to reject any form of general theory. "In the question of methods concerned with reconstruction of specific situations rather than in any refinements in the general concepts of institution, individuality, state, freedom, law, order, progress, etc., lies the true impact of philosophical reconstruction" (*Reconstruction*, p. 193).

The chief difficulty with this argument is that it is hard to see where a study of society might begin or end. One of the weaknesses of this side of pragmatism is that it unnecessarily limits our knowledge by making impossible any theory of society, as opposed to specific case studies.[8] But a general theory of the relationships among the various parts of society can be as important for guiding action as any specific hypothesis geared to solving a particular problem. Dewey imagines men always confronting distinct problems. But problems overlap, and reality does not lend itself easily to being broken into atomistic units, especially in the world of political practice. Theorizing and thinking about society and politics are impossible without using concepts abstract enough to relate propositions about different phenomena in some coherent order. Not surprisingly, Dewey's strictures against general theories often are ignored in his own work. At times he may take a position of crude empiricism and imagine the facts speaking for themselves. But more commonly, he recognizes the need for concepts to order and interpret the facts. Therefore, we find him substituting his own universal concepts for those he rejects. He is prone to emphasize the characteristic features of men's activities, rather

---

8. Sabine argues that this focus on particular case studies has been Dewey's major influence on political science ("Pragmatic Approach to Political Science," pp. 856–86).

than the specific activities themselves. Such universal terms as "association" and "communication" are central to much of his analysis.

Dewey's stress on the need for ideas to direct experience advances a more positive role for philosophy and a considerably more liberal view of the function of theory. "The need for large and generous ideas in the direction of life was never more urgent than in the confusion of tongues, beliefs and purposes that characterizes present life. . . . The meaning of science in terms of science, in terms of knowledge of the actual, may well be left to science itself. Its meaning in terms of the great human uses to which it may be put, its meaning in the service of possibilities of secure value, offers a field for exploration which cries out from very emptiness. . . . Such a philosophy would have a wide field of criticism before it. But its critical mind would be directed against the domination exercised by prejudice, narrow interest, routine custom and the authority which issues from institutions apart from the human ends they serve" (*Quest for Certainty*, pp. 311-12). However, Dewey always combines his enthusiasm for philosophy's role in criticizing and evaluating the overall consequences of men's actions and beliefs with his concern for solving specific problems. The philosopher, he insists, must also be "helping men solve problems in the concrete by supplying them hypotheses to be used and tested in projects of reform" (*Reconstruction*, p. 192).

Dewey's argument about general theory is clearly ambivalent. He stresses the need for broad interpretative ideas in social life and warns simultaneously of the dangers in not constantly referring a thought to the concrete and specific situation. Joseph Ratner has suggested that what Dewey rejects is analysis of "problems in general" but not the study of "general problems."[9] In one sense, this is a useful distinction. Dewey regards most social and political theories as nonempirical because they treat problems in abstract terms. He is a behaviorist in this sense: All ideas must be grounded empirically; they must refer to, and be derived from, the behavior of men. Dewey views certain problems as perennial: education and socialization, order and change, and other issues which

9. Ratner, "Dewey's Conception of Philosophy," in *Philosophy of John Dewey,* ed. Schilpp, pp. 49-73, hereafter cited by title only.

cluster around the activities of the community as it attempts to control social forces. Such problems can be considered as empirical but general. They set the agenda for Dewey's social and political theory.

Nevertheless, his instrumentalism often leaves one wondering at what point theorizing becomes too much or too little. Dewey's admiration for scientific method and concrete inquiry often runs head-on into his desire to provide a comprehensive, integrated account of the consequences of men's actions. Managing this tension becomes a major problem in his social and political thought.

Instrumentalism is Dewey's answer, of course, to the need for a reconstruction of philosophy. Instrumentalism is an account of the logic of inquiry which, in turn, is tied closely to a particular theory of reality. As part of his criticism of those dualisms separating knowing and acting, Dewey must deal with the bifurcation of the universe into quantitative and qualitative properties that is part of the scientific outlook. Science, Dewey acknowledges, is concerned exclusively with the primary properties of an object—mass, motion, velocity, and so forth. Much of the success of science depends on abstracting from reality those features capable of being expressed in abstract and quantitative terms. Science makes reality less complex and more manageable by expressing relationships in quantitative terms which can be studied mathematically. As part of his effort, the scientist excludes the qualitative, or tertiary, properties of an object from consideration. The scientist does not describe a table as a table but as "a swarm of molecules in motions of specified velocities and accelerations" (Quest for Certainty, p. 238). Relegation of the qualitative dimensions of experience—attractiveness, usefulness, value—to the mere subjective is the challenge posed by science's treatment of reality. In particular, it challenges the pragmatic account of knowing as an activity which transforms a problematic situation into a settled one. It suggests that the problematic is only a matter of opinion.

Dewey's first response to this challenge is to argue that scientific abstractions are only a partial description of reality. When the scientist talks about a table, he is interested in it apart from any use it may have. Indeed, he is not interested in the table *as* a table. But a table is a useful object and any full account must include a description of those uses. A scientist describes a table as an object made up of particles between which there are large holes; but when he sits down to dine, the table has no holes. Dewey's position is that both understandings of the table—its primary properties and its practical uses— are part of its meaning. The scientific outlook is not wrong, but it is incomplete (*Quest for Certainty*, pp. 239-40).

Having rejected the view that scientific abstractions are equivalent to the reality of nature, Dewey is prepared to argue that the qualitative features of an experience are equally real and objective. As Somjee rightly points out, Dewey "does not use the term 'experience' in a possessive sense, as in 'my experience' or 'your experience.'" Instead, Dewey talks about experience as "experience of the environment." Experience is "primarily a process of undergoing; a process of standing something; of suffering and passion, of affection, in the literal sense of these words." Such experiences take place within an "environing medium, not in a vacuum." It is in the interaction between man and his environment, and not in some psychic realm, that we discover the conditions and qualities of experience. If the qualitative parts of experience were not real, then it would be possible to change an unpleasant circumstance into a happy one simply by changing your mind. But it is a form of madness to imagine that a dishonest man is honest or that a coward is courageous. "Honesty, chastity, malice, peevishness, courage, triviality, industry, irresponsibility are not private possessions of a person. They are working adaptations of personal capacities with environing forces." Similarly, a problematic situation is one marked by such normative features as doubt, perplexity, and dissatisfaction. But Dewey argues that "It is the situation that has these traits. We are doubtful because the situation is inherently doubtful. The problematic in experience is part of a unified existential situation. Qualities such as pain and uncertainty are parts of experience; they are felt but they are not mere feelings. Inquiry must, therefore, aim to actually modify existing conditions; the problem cannot be resolved by merely mental processes."[10]

10. Somjee, *Political Theory of John Dewey*, p. 13; Dewey, "Need for Recovery of Philosophy," in *On Experience, Nature, and Freedom*, pp. 24, 25-26; *Human*

The implications of Dewey's theory of reality have been described in some detail by Hans Reichenbach. "Dewey does not only want to establish knowledge in a better and more solid form. What he intends, and perhaps to a greater extent, is establishing the sphere of values, of human desires and aims, on the same basis and in an analogous form as the system of knowledge. If concrete things as immediately experienced are the truly 'real' world, if the scientific thing is nothing but an auxiliary logical construction for better handling of the 'real' things, then ethical and esthetical valuations are 'real' properties of things as well as are the purely cognitive properties, and it is erroneous to separate valuations as subjective from cognitive properties as objective. In persuasive language and in ever-renewed form Dewey insists upon this outcome of his theory, the establishment of which seems to be the motive force in the work of this eminently practical mind, 'practical' to be taken in both its implications as 'moral' and 'directed towards action'. . . . If the pragmatist considers secondary and tertiary qualities as real he does so because he wants to establish esthetics and ethics as aspects of reality comparable to physics; because he wants to show that esthetic and moral judgments are statements of physical facts. It is the desire to establish objective esthetics and ethics, as opposed to subjective conceptions of esthetics and ethics, which stand behind the pragmatist's theory of reality."[11] Reichenbach is concerned primarily with the implications of the pragmatic account of reality for a theory of ethics. But that account affects equally the pragmatist version of truth. Since knowing is literally something that we do, Dewey follows Peirce and James in maintaining that the truth of an idea can be measured by its consequences when acted upon. In Dewey's words, this means that "If ideas, meanings, conceptions, notions, theories, systems, are instrumental to an active reorganization of the given environment, to a removal of some specific trouble and perplexity, then the test of their validity and value lies in accomplishing this work. If they succeed in their office they are reliable, sound,

---

Nature and Conduct, pp. 19, 50-54; Quest for Certainty, pp. 227, 232-33; Dewey's emphasis.

11. Reichenbach, "Dewey's Theory of Science," in Philosophy of John Dewey, pp. 162-63, 178.

valid, good, true. If they fail to clear up confusion, uncertainty and evil when they are acted upon, then are they false. Confirmation, corroboration, verification lie in works, consequences."[12] The maxim that truth is what works has been criticized widely and even ridiculed by pragmatism's opponents. When William James argued that the test of an idea was its "cash-value" in practice, critics charged that the pragmatist philosophy reflected the American preoccupation with what could make money. When again with his characteristic penchant for provocative language, James titled his essay on the justification of religious faith *The Will to Believe*, a later critic would identify pragmatism with the "will-to-power" politics of fascism. To the first charge, Dewey responded aptly that it resembled an explanation of the dualisms in French philosophy in terms of a supposed French predilection for keeping a mistress and a wife.[13] However, the complaint that pragmatism is an apologia for what works has generally stuck; the popular equation of the pragmatic with the practical or utilitarian reflects the pragmatist's apparent vulnerability on this point.

The quarrel over the epistemological standing of the pragmatist theory of truth can best be left to philosophers and logicians. The primary concern here is with those factors circumscribing Dewey's insistence that performance counts or that consequences measure an idea's validity. First, Dewey always locates the knowing activity in some interaction between man and his environment. When Dewey says that an idea "works," "succeeds," or "satisfies," we must not lose sight of the temporal process involved in knowing. The subject matter of inquiry is always some problematic situation as distinguished from "non-reflectional experiences." Dewey argues that pragmatism would not be misunderstood if knowing were viewed as a dynamic process. "The change made in things by the self in knowing is not immediate and, so to say, cross-sectional. It is longitudinal—in the redirection given to changes already going on. Its analogue is found in the changes which take place in the development of, say, iron ore into a watchspring, not in those of the miracle of transubstantiation. For the static, cross-sectional,

12. Dewey, *Reconstruction*, p. 156; *Essays in Experimental Logic*, chap. 8.
13. Dewey, "Experience, Knowledge and Value," in *Philosophy of John Dewey*, p. 527.

non-temporal relation of subject and object, the pragmatic hypothesis substitutes apprehension of a thing in terms of the results in other things which it is tending to effect."[14]

Responding directly to his critics, Dewey insists that the "needs and conditions of the problem out of which the idea, the purpose and method of action arises" alone are relevant to determining the truth of an idea.[15] What works, the consequences which count, are those that come at the end of the process of inquiry.

When Dewey describes truth as satisfaction of the "conditions prescribed by the problem," he is building upon his account of experience as an existential situation. It is easy to follow him on this point, if we think of an astronomer searching for a better way to observe a celestial body. As an astronomer, he does not create arbitrarily the need for a better means of observation; the problem and the need arise from the experience he is undergoing. In solving his problem, what works is not merely a matter of a change in desire: His idea must be tried. Dewey's more difficult point is his apparent belief that there is no fundamental difference between the experience of the astronomer and the experience of, say, the consumer who demands some form of protective legislation. The problematic condition experienced by the exploited consumer is equally an objective function of his experience as a consumer. Whether or not this analogy is satisfactory, it explains Dewey's confidence in "standard deliberate inquiry" as a method for resolving social conflict, much the same as science has dealt successfully with natural problems. This confidence and its underpinnings will be assessed at those points where Dewey's philosophical system translates into a political technology.

The Meaning of Naturalism

Instrumentalism applied to ethics becomes the doctrine of naturalism. It is Dewey's solution for cutting through the confusion created by the disjunction between the way men

14. Dewey, "Need for Recovery of Philosophy," in On Experience, Nature, and Freedom, p. 63.
15. See Dewey, "Experience, Knowledge and Value," in Philosophy of John Dewey, pp. 517-608.

formulate beliefs about the structure of society and the way they formulate judgments about the desirable or valuable. The major points in Dewey's theory of ethics are not difficult to state. As an opponent of absolute rationalism, he insists that philosophy has no unique understanding of the good. Philosophy must begin with men's actual beliefs about what is good and bad, desirable and undesirable, as its subject matter. But Dewey is not an ethical relativist. There are, he argues, objective criteria for making value decisions. He distinguishes first between the "enjoyed and the enjoyable, the desired and the desirable, the satisfying and the satisfactory." While the ethical doctrine of hedonism maintains that anything desired is a good, Dewey argues that "the fact that something is desired only raises the question of its desirability; it does not settle it" (*Quest for Certainty*, p. 260). The difference between a genuine and a specious good, according to Dewey's ethics, turns on reflection or criticism. Dewey's naturalism is an attempt to reduce judgments of values to judgments of facts so that intelligence can solve moral problems the way it solves other problems.

The valuation process is similar to any situation characterized by reflective thought: (1) a present condition is judged unsatisfactory and is assigned a negative value; (2) a comparatively positive value is assigned some future set of conditions; and (3) these two acts are linked by some intermediary set of propositions meant to guide the transition from the present situation to the desired one. Although this process describes the behavior of someone engaging in value choices, Dewey acknowledges that it does not say anything about the worth of a particular value judgment.[16] What, then, is the philosopher to do about value choices? Philosophers usually respond in one of two ways: they claim that "reason" can discover a hierarchy of absolute goods, or they resort to complete egoism or subjectivism and claim that anything a man desires is a good. Idealism or absolute rationalism, Dewey argues, claims too much for philosophy; subjectivism claims too little. What philosophy has is a method; it can aid men in clarifying their value judgments by bringing the tools of critical intelligence to the valuational process. "The suggestion almost imperatively follows that

16. Dewey, *Theory of Valuation*, pp. 12–13.

escape from the defects of transcendental absolutism is not to be had by setting up as values enjoyments that happen anyhow, but in defining value by enjoyments which are the consequences of intelligent action. Without the intervention of thought, enjoyments are not values but problematic goods, becoming values when they re-issue in a changed form from intelligent behavior" (*Quest for Certainty*, p. 259).

Dewey argues that a moral choice is something occurring within a problematic situation. He emphasizes the conditions which create the problem, not the distinctly moral issues involved in the situation. The only way reason can make a difference in value choices is if men treat moral problems foremost *as* problems. Dewey's emphasis is on the practical effects of moral choices. "To say that something satisfies is to report something as an isolated finality. To assert that it is satis*factory* is to define it in its connections and interactions. The fact that it pleases or is immediately congenial poses a problem to judgment. How shall the satisfaction be rated? Is it a value or is it not? Is it something to be prized and cherished, *to be* enjoyed? . . . To declare something satis*factory* is to assert that it meets specifiable conditions. It is, in effect, a judgment that the thing 'will do.' It involves a prediction; it contemplates a future in which the thing will continue to serve; it *will* do. It asserts a consequence the thing will actively institute; it will *do*" (*Quest for Certainty*, pp. 260–61, Dewey's emphasis).

Moral activity is thus very much a matter of intelligent problem solving. This means that the moral order is not something settled once and for all but something constantly changing and dependent on the deeds of men. In *Ethics*, Dewey and James Tufts offered a variety of reasons for studying the history of morals, but two were given special emphasis. First, they felt that such a review exposed as outdated many present standards and ideals. Since moral principles are propositions "which describe and define certain things as good, fit, or proper in a definite existential relation," some of these may apply to present conditions and some may not. Second, both men were convinced that ethics is above all a practical matter. "In this theater of man's life it is reserved for God and the angels to be lookers on. Man must act; and he must act well or ill, rightly or wrongly" (pp. 4–5). The chief merit of naturalism is its awareness that ethics makes a claim to guiding men's conduct, and that moral principles, therefore, should be formed with that claim and task in mind.

Dewey's insistence that ethics does matter and that moral theory must link its analysis to everyday problems is a needed addition to a study dominated often by either homiletics or abstruse reasoning. His theory of ethics is essentially an insistence that rigid habits be replaced by critical intelligence and that ideals and values be examined constantly in light of changing historical conditions. In short, his ethics bids men first to examine the meaning of their values in terms of probable consequences and then to act accordingly.

In Dewey's naturalism, all objectively true statements are also normative; judgments of values and judgments of facts are combined by reason. Certainly, a great deal can be said for this argument. Men's efforts to resolve moral problems are aided greatly by knowledge of the interconnections among social forces and by careful consideration of the relationship between means and ends. Dewey reminds us that moral perplexities are never completely settled; they are recurring issues that require continuous study of specific relationships in order to be handled intelligently. But critics have pointed out repeatedly that Dewey's theory of ethics cannot really account for moral obligation. One objection to his theory is made by reducing it to the absurd: If Dewey is correct in maintaining that de facto statements are also de jure, this would have to apply to all true statements. But to say that a table is brown and will be seen as such by everyone with normal vision does not impose an obligation on anyone. Yet Dewey's theory seems to commit him to the affirmation of such an obvious absurdity.[17] The objection is that naturalism neglects or confuses the difference between rational judgment and the judgment or feeling of moral obligation. A moral dilemma confronts a person not because some obstacle is present, or because he needs more information, but because there is a genuine conflict between values. For example, a man faced with the decision of whether or not to obey his government's order to report for military duty may make a

17. This is the argument made by White in *Social Thought*, pp. 214–18. For a summary of the major criticism of Dewey's naturalistic ethics, see Cook, "Inquiry into Ethical Foundations of Democracy," chap. 5.

totally rational judgment about the effects of service on his life, the merits of present government policy, and the costs to himself and others of serving or not serving. But this information does not really settle the question of what he should do. He is not confronted with a problematic situation because he lacks knowledge about a set of conditions, but because he must decide between the competing values of obedience and disobedience. In this context, it is easy to see the significance of one writer's objection to Dewey's ethics: "In repeatedly deferring to the 'needs' of a not-yet-arrived 'situation' the issue of the ground of moral choice is evaded rather than met."[18] When a moral dilemma is present *now*, the future "truth" or "value" of an action is no test at all.

As part of his theory of right conduct, Dewey introduces a second standard—community norms or social pressures. He emphasizes the social context within which individuals must act. While an individual is still personally responsible for the morality of his actions, we cannot ignore the place of social relationships in influencing his choices. In *Human Nature and Conduct*, Dewey writes, "Why, indeed, acknowledge the authority of Right? If a man lived alone in the world there might be some sense in the question 'Why be moral?' were it not for one thing: No such question would then arise. As it is, we live in a world where other persons live too. Our acts affect them. They perceive these effects, and react upon us in consequence. Because they are living beings they make demands upon us for certain things from us. They approve and condemn—not in abstract theory but in what they do to us. The answer to the question 'Why not put your hand in the fire?' is the answer of fact. If you do your hand will be burnt. The answer to the question why acknowledge the right is of the same sort. For Right is only an abstract name for the multitude of concrete demands in action which others impress upon us, and of which we are obliged, if we would live, to take some account. Its authority is the exigency of their demands, the efficacy of their insistencies. There may be good ground for the contention that in theory the idea of right is subordinate to that of the good, being a statement of the course proper to attain good. But in fact it signifies the totality of social pressures exercised upon us to

18. McDonald, *Western Political Theory*, p. 560.

induce us to think and desire in certain ways. *Hence the right can in fact become the road to the good only as the elements that compose this unremitting pressure are enlightened, only as social relationships become themselves reasonable"* (pp. 297-98, emphasis added). Dewey's thesis is that moral progress, the good life, depends on two closely related developments. Intelligence must effect a transformation and reorganization of men's relationships and beliefs when these have become outdated and oppressive. But at the same time, every individual is part of a vast network of social relationships; the environment must be refashioned also to make possible a particular type of intelligence or social education. In other words, there are no one-way streets in society; the education of man, his use of intelligence, also requires the simultaneous transformation of the environment which shapes him.[19]

Dewey treats both ideas and ethics as a form of interaction between man and his environment. The spread of intelligence and the transformation of the environment progress together via problem solving. A concrete difficulty calls forth ideas for removing a problem and leads to that action which transforms experience. Since it is not all one piece and contains forces which create problems, the environment also leads to the education of man. But education can be halting, wasteful, and oppressive, if men fail deliberately to seek understanding of the demands of changing conditions. The problem of education is thus the major problem of the human situation. Intelligence is effective in removing social ills only when it has become widespread among the members of a society. And it is Dewey's contention that through education and communication, men

19. Dewey's statements about community norms and social pressures as giving authority to the notions of right and wrong have been criticized for their reactionary, or at least conservative, implications. For instance, Elliott's argument that fascism represented a "pragmatic revolt in politics" rests partly on the contention that pragmatism justifies whatever "works" and subordinates reason to the "reign of social forces." This neglects what Dewey says about the necessity for transforming social institutions to make them "reasonable." Social pressures probably do account for much of the individual's sense of what is right. Dewey contends that this makes it all the more important to find ways to insure that the habits or rules of conduct enforced by these pressures are moral ones. It would be helpful if he were more attentive to the implications of his remarks, but this is no reason for ignoring what he intends for this ethical theory (*Pragmatic Revolt in Politics*).

come to recognize their common interest in solving certain problems. Obligation, in other words, is a function of membership in a particular type of community: one committed to the common good. By the common good, however, Dewey does not mean a specific end; rather, he means a society which measures moral progress by the continuing growth and development of individual personality. This, in turn, requires social cooperation.

Since ethics deals with activity, Dewey advocates growth as the only correct moral goal. Growth is the activity which resolves a present problem, while opening up the possibility for resolving other problems as they arise. Morals are not a separate realm but "part and parcel of a normal life process." Progress in morals comes with that "kind of expansion in meaning which is consequent upon observations of the condition and outcome of conduct" (Human Nature and Conduct, p. 259). "The process of growth, of improvement and progress, rather than the static outcome and result, becomes the significant thing. . . . The end is no longer a terminus or limit to be reached. It is the active process of transforming this existent situation. Not perfection as a final goal, but the ever-enduring process of perfecting, maturing, refining is the aim in living. . . . Growth itself is the only moral 'end'" (Reconstruction, p. 177).

To clarify his meaning, Dewey applies his ethical criteria to a specific situation. He points out that the factory worker too often produces ends in which he "has no share in forming and in which as such, apart from his wage, he has no interest." There is no meaningful connection here between a man's activity and its purposes. The creative and intelligent activity which constitutes morals is therefore impossible (Human Nature and Conduct, pp. 135-38). If he is to develop, man must participate actively in controlling the decisions which shape his life. Naturalism's conception of the good cannot be understood apart from instrumentalism's emphasis on the values of reasoned action.

Like other difficulties, moral problems do not occur in a vacuum but within some interaction between the individual and his environment. Human Nature and Conduct, written in 1922, explores such "interactions"—a term Dewey substitutes for the more familiar concepts of the individual and society. To examine the character of these interactions and the associated individual, he begins with the notion of habit and defines it very broadly. "The essence of habit is an acquired predisposition to *ways* or modes of response, not to particular acts except as, under special conditions, these express a way of behaving. Habit means special sensitiveness or accessibility to certain classes of stimuli, standing predilections and aversions, rather than bare recurrence of specific acts. It means will" (Dewey's emphasis). Habits define the self; e.g., character is the "interpenetration of habits," customs are the collective habits of a group, and finally, habits or customs are a major cause of the feeling of moral obligation (pp. 40–41). Dewey's concept of habits is linked to his rejection of individualism. A person's nature is not original but equivalent to those habits acquired under social influences. "Some activity proceeds from a man; then it sets up reactions in the surroundings. Others approve, disapprove, protest, encourage, share and resist. Even letting a man alone is a definite response. Envy, admiration and imitation are complicities. Neutrality is non-existent. Conduct is always shared; this is the difference between it and a physiological process. It is not an ethical 'ought' that conduct *should* be social. It *is* social, whether good or bad" (p. 19, Dewey's emphasis).

Morality finally comes down to the question of which habits or forms of conduct the individual possesses. It is impossible, therefore, to talk sensibly about the morality of conduct apart from an inquiry into how the social environment forms a person's character. By viewing morals as social, Dewey's naturalism and instrumentalism are linked. Morality is another form of problem solving. "There is seen to be but one issue involved in all reflection upon conduct: The rectifying of present troubles, the harmonizing of present incompatibilities by projecting a course of action which gathers into itself the meaning of them all. The recognition of the true psychology also reveals to us the nature of good or satisfaction. Good consists in the meaning that is experienced to belong to an activity when conflict and entanglement of various incompatible impulses and habits terminate in a unified orderly release in action" (*Human Nature and Conduct*, p. 196). Habits are necessary and useful guides to conduct, but they also can become outdated or "arrested" as the natural and social environments change. But the individual cannot suddenly become an isolated atom; his rules of conduct or modes of behavior, and his moral growth, depend on reform of social institutions. When we look at the problem of morality from the side of society, the issue becomes an "engineering issue, the establishment of arts of education and social guidance" (p. 11).

Problem solving, or moral growth, is therefore a social, not an individual, task. The "individual by himself can do little to regulate the conditions which will render important values more secure." This requires a society where cooperation, rather than conflict, characterizes men's relationships. "Every maladjustment in relations among these institutions and associated activities means loss and friction in the relations between individuals; and thereby introduces defect, division, and restriction into the various powers which constitute an individual. All harmonious cooperation among them means a fuller life and greater freedom of thought and action for the individual person." Only social ends are truly reasonable. They alone enable the individual to organize his acts to account for all the consequences implicit in them. "In form, the true good is thus an inclusive or expanding end. In substance, the only end which fulfills these conditions is the social good."[20] Individual moral growth, or individuality, is not possible apart from the development of reasonable social relationships and institutions that form a community. And it is from this perspective that Dewey's later writings inquire into the meaning of economic and political arrangements.

20. Dewey, *Quest for Certainty*, p. 40; Dewey and Tufts, *Ethics* pp. 430, 386.

3. Political Education

Upon some generous souls of the
eighteenth century there dawned the
idea that the cause of the indefinite
improvement of humanity and the
cause of the little child are insep-
arably bound together.

Ethics

THE HISTORY of American political philosophy can be told
partly in terms of the country's attitude toward popular education.[1] An educated citizenry has been viewed as a safeguard of
the subject's liberty or, conversely, as protection against the
excesses of popular rule, both as a method of reducing class
distinctions and as a way of educating each man for his place.
With shifts in the estimation of what can and cannot be
expected of the educated or enlightened citizen, democratic
theory also has undergone revision.[2] Such concerns are as old as

1. See Welter, *Popular Education and Democratic Thought.*
2. These shifts in political thought, however, are not simply historical.
Indeed, the issues posed by the connections between education and politics, and
the educational impact of politics, usually come to the fore whenever schools of
thought offer varying interpretations of the meaning of citizenship and political
participation. For instance, much of the current political science discussion
about the merits of American politics and how to study the political system is a
debate over the theoretical and normative utility of notions such as the rational
and responsible citizen. See Bachrach, *Theory of Democratic Elitism.*

Plato's account of the state as a schoolmaster for teaching subjects virtue.

To inquire into an author's writings on political education is to ask, then, what type of character he deems necessary for a particular political system to work. And Dewey probably comes closer than most writers to employing educational theory as a vehicle for reconstructing democratic theory. This theme is pursued in its more political contexts in later chapters. For now, a discussion of Dewey's educational theory will provide some further substantive elaboration of his vision of the good society.

DEMOCRATIC EDUCATION

The major features of Dewey's philosophy point to education or, more broadly, to intelligence as the major means for improving man's condition. As C. Wright Mills has said, Dewey's conception of problems as maladjustments between man and the environment makes "man's use of intelligence to work 'his' way out of the difficulties 'he' faces the solution to all problems." Dewey insists, for example, that underlying all forms of conflict between men there are actually objective disharmonies between men's beliefs and/or practices on the one hand, and the demands of the environment on the other. Beliefs formed by habit, accidental circumstances, propaganda, or personal and class bias, are to be replaced by beliefs resulting from rational inquiry.[3] Dewey's confidence in the power of intelligence to make a major difference in social life is tied to his argument that scientific inquiry and common sense do not differ in principle; they are on a continuum. Scientific procedure is a style of thought and mode of activity equivalent to certain common-sense rules for determining the validity of any idea or hypothesis. Every man, therefore, is capable potentially of guiding his affairs in light of "scientific" knowledge. In *Reconstruction in Philosophy*, Dewey expresses one of the dominant concerns of classical democratic theory: "Government, business, art, religion, all social institutions have a meaning, a purpose. That purpose is to set free and to develop the capacities of human individuals without respect to race, sex, class or economic

3. Mills, *Sociology and Pragmatism*, p. 382; Dewey, *Quest for Certainty*, p. 265.

status. And this is all one with saying that the test of their value is the extent to which they educate every individual into the full stature of his possibility. Democracy has many meanings, but if it has a moral meaning, it is found in resolving that the supreme test of all political institutions and industrial arrangements shall be the contribution they make to the all-around growth of every member of society" (*Reconstruction*, p. 186). On the other hand, society is also shaped by the direct and indirect education given its members. And formal education does play a special role in equipping newer members of society with the habits of mind and attitudes which will enable them to reconstruct and reorganize social institutions as changing conditions demand. Dewey thus conceives of the school as a society within a larger society: A correct education demands that the school prepare students for their role as rational citizens. The educational experience itself must be democratic; an authoritarian situation in the classroom discourages those very habits of mind and those attitudes necessary for a democratic citizenry. But the larger society in turn must be thought of as a school, since its institutions also have an educative impact.

Since Dewey's theory of education is contained largely within his philosophy of ideas and experience, its essential features can be summarized easily. Most conceptions of education, he argues, suffer from a common defect: They separate knowing and doing. In *Democracy and Education*, published in 1916, he writes, "In schools, those under instruction are too customarily looked upon as acquiring knowledge as theoretical spectators, minds which appropriate knowledge by direct energy of intellect. The very word pupil has almost come to mean one who is engaged not in having fruitful experiences but in absorbing knowledge directly. Something which is called mind or consciousness is severed from the physical organs of activity. The former is then thought to be purely intellectual and cognitive; the latter to be an irrelevant and intruding physical factor. The intimate union of activity and undergoing its consequences which leads to recognition of meaning is broken; instead we have two fragments: mere bodily action on one side, and meaning directly grasped by 'spiritual' activity on the other" (pp. 140–41).

In contrast, Dewey contends that a person learns by doing. "It is through what we do in and with the world that we read its meaning and measure its value." This is the theme of *The School and Society*, Dewey's first major book on education (p. 17). In this work his arguments often draw on his own experiences as a child in Vermont. In a small, self-sufficient community, such needs as clothing and lighting are produced by several people working actively together. The individual participates in such processes from beginning to end; his understanding is a function of his participation and concern. Since the individual has to actively grasp the relationship between means and ends, such experiences are truly educative.

Dewey does not imagine that today's industrial system can be patterned after the practices of a simpler age. Nor does he underestimate the benefits produced by technological improvements. But he does believe it is possible to enlarge greatly the individual's participation in those activities which influence the direction of his life. Education has a special task to teach a person to seek out the connections between his activities and their ends. In short, the development of mind is part of a person's experiences. In the classroom, the teacher's role is to engage the student's original interests and to arrange for him to have experiences that through active participation will develop his powers of observation and his ability to order means and ends. It is this directive, guiding role which defines the vital office of the teacher.[4]

Dewey's educational philosophy is also a philosophy of man in society. The human condition is problematic in that each individual must be educated for society; indeed, society exists only by virtue of transmitting from one generation to the next its ideals, hopes, expectations, and traditions. Life means becoming part of a tradition, a shared culture. But becoming part of a tradition can be liberating or restrictive. To educate the individual to become part of society without being cast into a rigid mold is the essence of the human situation. Dewey's educational doctrine maintains that education is its own end—

---

4. Despite the seemingly ineradicable view that Dewey urges the teacher to leave the student alone to pursue his own interests his own way, Dewey himself insists frequently upon the teacher's responsibility to guide the student's activities. For example, see "Individuality and Freedom," in *Intelligence in the Modern World*, pp. 619-27.

the growth of the learner. "When it is said that education is development, everything depends upon *how* development is conceived. Our net conclusion is that life is development, and that developing, growing is life. Translated into its educational equivalents, that means (i) that the educational process has no end beyond itself; it is its own end; and that (ii) the educational process is one of continual reorganizing, reconstructing, transforming" (*Democracy and Education*, pp. 49-50, Dewey's emphasis).

As a method of "continual reorganizing," scientific inquiry and education become allied with social reform. Education aims at developing the critical faculties of the child. The student does not simply accept society's traditions; he must examine constantly the beliefs and the nature of social institutions. This theory of formal education is clearly political. It sets out to produce individuals who are skeptical of time-honored verities and committed to experimentalism in social action. Dewey often describes education as a process of "life-adjustment." The phrase is unfortunate, because it conveys an image of the individual adjusting his desires totally in response to the environment. Quite the contrary. "Adjustment," Dewey writes, "must be understood in its active sense of *control* of means for achieving ends" and as the "ability to effect subsequent changes in the environment" (*Democracy and Education*, p. 46, Dewey's emphasis). The environment must be adjusted to the individual.

Dewey's argument that education is growth has been the source of endless criticism. Critics have charged that "progressive education, although often immensely fertile and ingenious concerning means, was futile and confused about ends; much of what it had to say about teaching methods was of the highest value, but it was quite unclear, often anarchic, about what these methods should be used to teach."[5] Dewey was not unaware of

5. Hofstadter, *Anti-Intellectualism*, p. 375. Hofstadter reviews many of the absurd practices, such as "life-adjustment" courses, introduced into school curricula as a result of progressive education. He is careful to point out also that many of these practices bear little relationship to Dewey's original ideas. Nevertheless, he does not excuse Dewey entirely. "If for 'Latin' one substitutes 'driver education' or 'beauty culture,' considering each as justified if it makes 'an immediate appeal,' one senses the game that later educators played with Dewey's principles. Dewey himself presumably would not have made such substitutions, but in his philosophy there are no barriers against making them" (p. 377).

such objections. He even wrote *Experience and Education* in 1938 as a mild rebuke to those adherents of the "new education" who were praising any and every interest and experience the student has. Elsewhere, he even went so far as to label "really stupid" the notion that the teacher must not provide any direction or suggest any ends for the student's activity.[6] In insisting that all education depends on experience, Dewey does not mean that there is no need for guidance in the classroom. "When external authority is rejected, it does not follow that all authority should be rejected, but rather that there is need to search for a more effective source of authority. Because the older education imposed the knowledge, methods, and the rules of conduct of the mature person upon the young, it does not follow, except upon the basis of the extreme *Either-Or* philosophy, that the knowledge and skill of the mature person has no directive value for the experience of the immature."[7] Indeed, if there is some difficulty with Dewey's theory, the most sensible charge would be that his criteria for distinguishing between educative and miseducative experiences are either wrong or too ambiguous. His own writings, however, provide no excuse for abandoning the attempt to draw such distinctions.

While some criticize Dewey for failing to provide a clear set of educational goals, others attack him for being too clear. In *The New Radicalism in America*, Christopher Lasch argues that Dewey's advice to educators to promote progressive social change simply means "substituting one set of values for another, progressive values for conservative ones." And he concludes that "the indoctrination remained" (p. 160). Unless we assume that all education is equivalent to indoctrination, Lasch's criticism clearly is wide of the mark. Indoctrination occurs when people adopt a belief system without being able to critically reconstruct its foundations, and when they remain ignorant of why they behave as they do. No educational system can be innocent of the implication that it conditions man's behavior and purposes. But what separates education from indoctrination is the ability of a person to perceive and understand the relationship between his beliefs and behavior.

6. See Ratner, "Dewey's Conception of Philosophy," in *Philosophy of John Dewey*, p. 624.

7. Dewey, *Experience and Education*, p. 21, Dewey's emphasis.

Dewey's point is that education necessarily involves the transmission of some cultural values. The transmission occurs in any case. He urges that educators be aware of this process and make an effort to alert the student to it. But neither teacher nor student can evade the necessity for attempting to distinguish between those values which are worthwhile and those which are worthless or even perverse.

In this context, there is nothing wrong with the doctrine that life is growth. Individuality is basically the development of one's ability to relate means and ends, to see the interconnections among social forces, and to foresee the consequences of some course of action. Individuality allows a person the opportunity and power to do for himself that which he desires. In Dewey's language, "choice *is* freedom." Without choice, a man is a "puppet" whose actions are controlled by external forces.[8] The intellectually free man is one who has the skills to cope with his problems; *his* purposes, not someone else's, direct his actions.

Nevertheless, Dewey often offers us a "method" when we expect some statement of ends or some indication of his position on a particular value conflict.[9] Although this is understandable in light of his ethical naturalism, it does not answer the objection that he often avoids profound moral discourse. Lee Cameron McDonald states the peculiarity of Dewey's position, pinpointing why many people have been dissatisfied with it: "Dewey was in a somewhat anomalous position, although perhaps he never fully realized it. He had certain values that in practice he advanced with vigor. . . . But philosophically he defended none of them; indeed, he could not consistently defend them, since his *sine qua non* was a methodology that deferred to the values of each emerging situation rather than some fixed catalogue of ends."[10]

But several things must be kept in mind when examining how Dewey handles values or ends. First is his theory of method. His discussion of educational techniques, for example, entails criteria for discriminating between the valuable and the worthless, between the educative and the miseducative. Intelligence or

8. Dewey, "Philosophies of Freedom," in *On Experience, Nature, and Freedom,* p. 262.

9. This is one of Mills' major complaints against Dewey. See *Sociology and Pragmatism,* p. 405.

10. McDonald, *Western Political Theory,* p. 565.

"method" is a standard for defending such values as individuality, communication, and community. These values cannot be separated from Dewey's understanding of intelligence. Second, Dewey believes and argues indirectly that a commitment to intelligence is accompanied by an awareness of shared problems and common needs. This is evident in his picture of the school as a "miniature community" serving as model for the larger society (Democracy and Education, p. 360).

Learning requires exchange of ideas, cooperative inquiries, and joint activities. This activity transforms the classroom into a community. Through participation and communication, the group develops some shared understandings and a sense of common purpose. Dewey foreshadows his discussion of how the problem of authority and freedom can be resolved in the larger democratic society by arguing that a classroom operating along democratic lines produces its own kind of discipline. This discipline is more intimate and tolerable than that imposed by outside authorities. In Experience and Education, Dewey states:

> Now, the general conclusion I would draw is that
> control of individual actions is effected by the whole
> situation in which individuals are involved, in which
> they share and of which they are cooperative or
> interacting parts. For even in a competitive game
> there is a certain kind of participation, of sharing
> in a common experience. Stated the other way
> around, those who take part do not feel that they
> are bossed by an individual person or are being
> subjected to the will of some outside superior
> person. . . .
> It may seem to be putting too heavy a load upon a
> single case to argue that this instance illustrates the
> general principle of social control of individuals
> without the violation of freedom. But if the matter
> were followed out through a number of cases, I think
> the conclusion that this particular instance does
> illustrate a general principle would be justified. . . .
> In all such cases it is not the will or desire of any
> one person which establishes order but the moving
> spirit of the whole group. The control is social, but
> individuals are parts of a community, not outside of
> it (pp. 53-54).

The school as a house of reason operating in accordance with the principle of cooperation provides Dewey with a model applicable to all areas of social life. In other words, Dewey's educational theory serves many of the functions that social and political theories usually perform. For instance, social, economic, and political ills are analyzed frequently in terms of knowledge and ignorance, scientific control, and planning versus drift. Conflict and power disparities are not overlooked; but it is held that intelligence operating within a social context, that is, within a community where men are bound together by a commitment to free communication, open inquiry, and cooperative ventures, can expose and remove social problems. A democratic education demands institutionalization of the experimental method in the classroom. Similarly, if the substance is to be part of the form, democracy requires the spread of the experimental attitude in politics. This, Dewey argues, is the only path to a community where the bonds of social unity enlarge, rather than circumscribe, the individual's freedom.

COMMUNITY

In 1888, Dewey wrote "The Ethics of Democracy," an essay embracing an organicist view of society. The essay defends democracy from the criticisms of Henry Maine by contrasting the organic view of society with Maine's atomistic conception of individuals. By treating society as an aggregation of numerical units, Maine indicts democracy—the rule of the multitude—as the most unstable and least desirable form of government. Since power is divided into small fragments and a multitude has no common will, an artificial unity has to be produced by the techniques of party and corruption.

In response, Dewey complains that Maine's criticism of democracy as a form of chaos is anachronistic. Maine's criticisms rest on a conception of society composed of individuals as isolated units. "The fact is, however, that the theory of the 'social organism,' that theory that men are not isolated non-social atoms, but are men only when in intrinsic relations to men, has wholly superseded the theory of men as an aggregate, as a heap of grains of sand needing some factitious mortar to put them into semblance of order. . . . Society, as a real whole, is the normal order, and the mass as an aggregate of isolated units is the fiction" (*Ethics of Democracy*, p. 7).

In interpreting society as an organism, Dewey assigns society a collective consciousness. He then attempts to relate the parts to the democratic whole by suggesting that the vote of the individual does not count as one but becomes the "expression of society through him." The "social organism weighs considerations and forms its consequent judgment." The individual only reaches perfection as part of the whole. He has "concentrated within himself [the] intelligence and will" of democracy. While Maine simply defines democracy as a form of government, Dewey follows the logic of his organicism by arguing that democracy is a moral association perfecting the organic relationship between individual and society. Dewey insists that individual personality is the highest value, but that the "individual is brought to reality in the state" (*Ethics of Democracy*, p. 19).

This early paper by Dewey is interesting primarily for two reasons. It indicates his early conviction that the distinction between the individual and society is false if taken as the starting point for a theory of politics. But it shows his uncertainty about what to do with the organic approach. He could not explain how individual will comes to be expressed in the will of the whole. The individual remains an ambiguous conception. He is part of the whole, Dewey repeats, even his anti-social acts are reflections of the whole; consequently, the "individual" becomes simply a synonym for "integral part of the whole."[11] In short, Dewey was clearer about why the mechanistic approach to society was wrong than he was about the positive implications of organic theory.

Since Dewey had not yet worked out his own social theory at the time of this paper, perhaps his account of society could not help but be skeletal. As his work progresses, he modifies considerably his organic conception of society, employing instead the theme of interdependency. We have already seen some of the results of his theme that analysis must proceed in terms of the interactions between man and the environment, the individual and the social. He explains human behavior by

11. See Somjee, *Political Theory of John Dewey*, p. 81.

reference to the determining influences of the environment. Both intelligent and ethical conduct are defined as essentially social: Each requires an awareness of and concern for the common interest. Dewey's argument that individual growth is bound to the reasonableness of social institutions indicates that he has not dropped completely the organic outlook. But the conception of a common good is worked out in terms of the common awareness of how actions affect public welfare. And in his educational theory, it is the principle of cooperation, the shared or joint quality of intelligence, which comes to the foreground. For a theory of society, he relies on the concepts "association" and "community."

For Dewey, that connections exist between men is a fact requiring no explanation. Whatever answer might be given to the question of how society started, Dewey maintains we would be right back where we started, with society as an established fact. "There is no problem in all history so artificial as that of how 'individuals' manage to form 'society.' The problem is due to the pleasure taken in manipulating concepts, and discussion goes on because concepts are kept from inconvenient contact with facts. The facts of infancy and sex have only to be called to mind to see how manufactured are the conceptions which enter into this particular problem."[12] In *Reconstruction in Philosophy*, he defines association as "any form of experience which is augmented and confirmed by being shared" (p. 205). Trade unions, churches, clubs, schools are examples. In effect, Dewey adopts a pluralistic view of society. "Groupings for promoting the diversity of goods that men share have become the real social units. They occupy the place which traditional theory has claimed either for mere isolated individuals or for the supreme and single political organization. Pluralism is well ordained in present political practice and demands a modification of hierarchical and monistic theory. Every combination of human forces that adds its own contribution to life has for that reason its own unique and ultimate worth" (p. 204).

This pluralist view of society resolves a conflict presented by Dewey's earlier organicist conception. Organicism was incompatible with the demand of his emerging methodology that

12. Dewey, *Human Nature and Conduct*, p. 56; see also *Public and Its Problems*, p. 23.

analysis focus on specific situations. To relate all aspects of society to a larger whole requires a level of abstraction prohibited by his theory of inquiry. The pluralist view creates no comparable difficulty for Dewey. The character of particular associations and the pattern of relationships among them are the proper focus of social and political theory. The problem of the part-whole relationship is replaced by a consideration of how the various parts interact.

On the other hand, Dewey's organicism is very much present still. By definition, associations are conjoint activities. Association, interdependency, and interactions are still the dominant social facts. But a developed or more mature approach to social theory is presented in this passage: "We cannot be satisfied with the general statement that society and the state is organic to the individual. The question is one of specific causations. Just what response does *this* social arrangement, political or economic, evoke, and what effect does it have upon the disposition of those who engage in it? Does it release capacity? If so, how widely? Among a few, with a corresponding depression in others, or in an extensive and equitable way? . . . Such questions as these . . . become the starting-points of inquiries about every institution of the community when it is recognized that individuality is not originally given but is created under the influences of associated life" (*Reconstruction*, pp. 197–98, Dewey's emphasis). To answer which type of environment unifies both aspects of personality—individuality and sociality—Dewey relies heavily on the idea of community.

Written in 1927, *The Public and Its Problems* argues that associations do not automatically constitute a community. Associations simply describe the fact of interdependence among men; they are a physical and organic necessity. In contrast, communal life is moral; it must be sustained intellectually, emotionally, and consciously. To form a community, each individual must participate actively in determining the values of the group. A community is thus a group of men engaged in collective action who share common beliefs and have some degree of common understanding. The family and the neighborhood reflect the ideal of community life. Such groups are small and knit closely. Personal power and participation count, and the individual learns to relate his desires to the needs of the group. "In its deepest and richest sense a community must always remain a matter of face-to-face intercourse" (p. 211).

While the characteristics of the local community cannot be reproduced totally on a larger scale, men do have common interests beyond the family, neighborhood, club, or some other group. These associations or local communities are exclusive and limited, but the idea of the larger community is inclusive and integrative. Dewey expresses this idea in *Democracy and Education.* Since he is criticized frequently for failure to provide any criteria for defining the good society, his statement is quoted at length. What is required, he writes, is some way to measure the worth of a given mode of social life.

> In seeking this measure, we have to avoid two extremes. We cannot set up, out of our heads, something we regard as an ideal society. We must base our conception upon societies which actually exist, in order to have any assurance that our ideal is a practicable one. But, as we have just seen, the ideal cannot simply repeat the traits which are actually found. The problem is to extract the desirable traits of forms of community life which actually exist, and employ them to criticize undesirable features and suggest improvement. Now in any social group whatever, even in a gang of thieves, we find some interest held in common, and we find a certain amount of interaction and cooperative intercourse with other groups. From these two traits we derive our standard. How numerous and varied are the interests which are consciously shared? How full and free is the interplay with other forms of association?. . .
>
> There is more than a verbal tie between the words common, community, and communication. Men live in a community in virtue of the things which they have in common; and communication is the way in which they come to possess things in common. What they must have in common in order to form a community or society are aims, beliefs, aspirations, knowledge—a common understanding—like-mindedness as the sociologists say (pp. 83, 4).

Dewey has often been accused of emphasizing techniques at the expense of ends or vision. But his idea of community argues that in the final analysis, technique cannot be separated from ends. Community—the end—is ultimately the means—communication. The *ways* men come to view their interests cannot be separated from what those interests will be. We have come full circle. The two standards used to evaluate the worth of social life are the extent to which interests are shared freely and the freedom with which groups interact. These are the educational ideals of free inquiry, cooperation, and communication, as transferred to the larger society.

The school, however, is only one path to community. Men do not form beliefs simply as a result of formal education. Nor are their interests dictated merely by the cool detachment of reason. The office of reason must be compared always to the place of power in ordering the relationships among men. In short, the analysis of education and community must be accompanied by the study of political and economic arrangements.

4. Politics and Social Control

Dewey RECOGNIZES that some people might interpret pragmatism's concern with the problems of men as an appeal to philosophers to "desert their studies, libraries, and laboratories" in order to influence the flow of events. But this is a caricature. The insistence that philosophy be relevant stems simply from Dewey's argument that "the need of a situation" is the measure of an idea's truth as well as its utility.[1] The chief advantage of focusing on experience as a central category in philosophy is that it directs attention to the role of ideas *in* experience. This approach undermines the attitude that rigorous thought is only possible when separated from a concern with concrete problems. When one grasps the importance of ideas for directing action, it becomes apparent that what is

1. Utility must not be interpreted narrowly, however. Sidney Hook puts it this way: "To begin with, when Dewey speaks of practice, he does not mean that philosophies must serve some immediate practical interest but that if they have meaning they commit us to some activity in relation to the world or situation which calls it forth. This activity or practice may be evaluated as useful or useless, good or bad; but the crucial question is whether such practice is relevant to the problem with which the philosopher is concerned, whether he is aware of its relevance, and is prepared to accept the consequences as evidence for or against the validity of his philosophy" (*John Dewey*, pp. 45-46). See also Kaplan, *Conduct of Inquiry*, pp. 43-44.

needed is more, not less, systematic thought. Dewey keeps reminding us that men must act in any case; as a guiding philosophy, instrumentalism permits the philosopher to serve truth through a concern with the problems of intelligently directed social action.[2]

POLITICAL ACTIVISM

Translated into a guide to political action, Dewey's philosophy encourages political activism. At its simplest level, this activism is rooted in Dewey's insistence that social philosophy be relevant to men's efforts to reorganize unsatisfactory experiences.

Dewey's account of science also fosters an activist attitude toward social problems. After all, instrumentalism is a philosophy of experimentation, control, directed change, and action. Scientific method applied to social forces means social engineering. In "Social Science and Social Control," Dewey states that social science can only be developed through social practice. "It is a complete error to suppose that efforts at social control depend upon the prior existence of a social science. The reverse is the case. The building up of social science, that is, of a body of knowledge in which facts are ascertained in their significant relations, is dependent upon putting social planning into effect. . . . Physical science did not develop because inquiries piled up a mass of facts about observed phenomena. It came into being when men intentionally experimented, on the basis of ideas and hypotheses, with observed phenomena to modify them and disclose new observations. This process is self-corrective and self-developing. Imperfect and even wrong hypotheses, when *acted upon*, brought to light significant phenomena which made improved ideas and improved experimentations possible. The change from a passive and accumulative attitude into an active and productive one is the secret revealed by the progress of physical inquiry" (*Intelligence in the Modern World*, pp. 951–52, Dewey's emphasis).

Dewey is not implying that the techniques of social experimentalism are exactly the same as those of the natural and physical sciences. It is the characteristic features of experi-

2. Dewey, *Individualism*, pp. 140–41.

mentalism which are applicable equally to questions in the physical or the social sciences. Science provides a certain pattern of problem-solving activity. It means paying close attention to the context within which some difficulty originates, keeping in mind the empirical phenomena represented by concepts and, most important, following what promises to be a successful plan for transforming the situation. This argument for more social "science" is a brief for more social control.

All the major features of Dewey's epistemology contribute to a manipulative and activist attitude: the stress on knowing through acting, his account of the problematic in experience, the doctrine of validating values by trying them out. The purpose of social and political action is nothing less than the creation of individuality. "Now it is true that social arrangements, laws, institutions are made for man, rather than that man is made for them; that they are means and agencies of human welfare and progress. But they are not means for obtaining something for individuals, not even happiness. They are means of *creating* individuals" (*Reconstruction*, p. 194, Dewey's emphasis).

Much of the appeal of Dewey's major teaching is its simplicity. Men should rely more on reason in dealing with social problems and with each other. Stated baldly, problems *are* problems with identifiable causes; within the limits of available knowledge, they have reasonable solutions. But Dewey recognizes that social conflicts are often about what is the right or the just thing to do, and that different economic, political, and social interests aggravate the conflict.[3] But this does not mean that experimentalism cannot be used to settle social conflicts. Value disputes can only be settled by a thoroughgoing naturalism; different interests can be reasonably adjusted only by appealing to what needs to be done to solve specific problems. Dewey urges that things be stated in such a way that reliance on intelligence, inquiry, or scientific method becomes the solution.

Naturalism avoids certain pitfalls common to most value disputes. First, it abandons moral "systems"—those abstract principles of good and evil that have no working relationship to actual conditions. Disputes over general notions of right and wrong can go on endlessly: Nothing empirical can check what is

3. Dewey, *Liberalism and Social Action*, p. 79.

said. This is why Dewey wants attention shifted to the particular difficulty at hand. "Most conflicts of importance are conflicts between things which are or have been satisfying, not between good and evil. And to suppose that we can make a hierarchical table of values at large once for all, a kind of catalogue in which they are arranged in an order of ascending or descending worth, is to indulge in a gloss on our inability to frame intelligent judgments in the concrete" (*Quest for Certainty*, p. 266).

For example, political disputes over "collectivism" versus "individualism" simply postpone inquiry into actual economic problems. But inquiry might "disclose certain specifiable conditions under which both of the methods vaguely pointed at by these words would operate to advantage." Bitter debates over abstract creeds are unnecessary if we substitute inquiry into the probable consequences of following this or that standard in a given situation.[4] "Where will regulation come from if we surrender familiar and traditionally prized values as our directive standards? Very largely from the findings of the natural sciences. For one of the effects of the separation drawn between knowledge and action is to deprive scientific knowledge of its proper service as a guide to conduct . . . a moral that frames judgments of value on the basis of consequences must depend in a most intimate manner upon the conclusions of science. For the knowledge of the relations between changes which enable us to connect things as antecedents and consequences *is* science" (*Quest for Certainty*, pp. 273-74, Dewey's emphasis). As Mills argues, Dewey uses "problem" as a surrogate for "value."[5] Conflicts of values and interests are transferred to the sphere of the problematic, since problems are objective and amenable to intelligent resolution in a way that questions of general values are not.

Naturalism and social experimentalism arbitrate social conflicts by postponing a decision about the desirable or valuable until a particular problem is understood. Goals are treated experimentally as an outgrowth of inquiry and communication. By not insisting that men agree about abstract principles, this argument makes it simpler for them to agree on practical

4. Dewey, *Freedom and Culture*, p. 118.
5. Mills, *Sociology and Pragmatism*, p. 411.

measures to remedy a specific abuse. After solving one problem, they can move on to the next. In *Freedom and Culture*, Dewey writes: "When general ideas are not capable of being continuously checked and revised by observation of what actually takes place, they are, as a mere truism, in the field of opinion. Clash of opinions is in that case the occasion for controversy, not, as is now the case in natural science, a location of a problem and an occasion for making further observations. If any generalization can be safely laid down about intellectual matters and their consequences, it is that the reign of opinion, and of controversial conflicts, is a function of absence of methods of inquiry which bring new facts to light and by so doing establish the basis for consensus of beliefs" (p. 116).

The type of social intelligence and political action which Dewey's philosophy recommends can be described best as a form of trial-and-error rationalism. As means and ends are linked through a process of trial and error, the ends as well as the means are adjusted to deal with the unfolding situation. Ends, Dewey argues, must be evaluated in light of the means necessary for achieving them. By their nature, ends are always plural. The end is that which is desired immediately; the means necessary to achieve the end are themselves immediate ends-in-view; and, finally, the specific end desired and the means necessary for achieving it are potential resources for, or obstacles to, other goals. Rational action is also "deliberate": It is guided by some plan which distinguishes it from "mere activity." However, this deliberateness is combined with "flexibility" to permit adjustments of both means and ends. Intelligent action is "practical"; it is neither bound by tradition nor tied to any fixed theory.[6]

Finally, reasonable conduct is also specific in operation. Both common sense and scientific research teach us that "every reflective problem and operation arises with reference to some *specific* situation, and has to subserve a *specific* purpose dependent upon its own occasion" (Dewey's emphasis).

6. Somjee, *Political Theory of John Dewey*, pp. 60–61; Dewey, *Theory of Valuation*, pp. 40–50, and *Human Nature and Conduct*, pp. 212, 228; for Dewey's account of the nature of trial-and-error rationalism, see *Democracy and Education*, pp. 104–6, 148–51.

Dewey's conceptions of both science and action narrow the range of rational conduct to the handling of concrete difficulties. "Scientific method would teach us to break up, to inquire definitely and with particularity, to seek solutions in the terms of concrete problems as they arise . . . for doing always means the doing of something in particular."[7] Somjee has argued that the rationalism of experimentalism is not that of some teleological process wherein action approximates some antecedent goal. Nor is it solely that of logical consistency. Rather, "its rationality is that of trial-and-error."[8] Dewey does not take us beyond the trial-and-error experience for two main reasons. First, it is impossible to foresee all the connections among social forces as these affect the outcome of some course of action. Second, this means that every idea must be tested in the real world by its consequences when acted upon.

Freedom and Culture, published originally in 1939, is the most systematic transfer of Dewey's model of trial-and-error rationalism to a theory of politics. Dewey argues three themes. He contends that the perspectives provided by a cultural approach to society and politics outlaw any but a pluralist and interactionist explanation of social change. The book is also a polemic against formal political theories in general and Marxism in particular. Finally, Dewey defends democratic processes in terms of their institutionalization of trial-and-error rationalism.

Dewey begins this book with a very broad conception of culture. Culture, he says, refers to all social relationships which influence men's habits and beliefs. Echoing an earlier argument from his more philosophical writings, he states that "no matter what is the native make-up of human nature, its working activities, those which respond to institutions and rules and which finally shape the pattern of the latter, are created by the whole body of occupations, interests, skills, beliefs that constitute a given culture." Thus, the problem of the relationship between *the* individual and *the* social is totally fanciful. At best, such philosophical dichotomies are functional distinctions within an experience. Experience itself always has an organic quality, such that the real problem is the *"ways of interaction"*

7. Dewey, *Studies in Logical Theory*, p. 50; *Individualism*, p. 165.
8. Somjee, *Political Theory of John Dewey*, p. 60.

between human nature and cultural conditions (pp. 7, 33, Dewey's emphasis).

This cultural perspective commits Dewey to a theory of social pluralism. He believes it is "pure willfulness if anyone pretending to a scientific treatment starts from any other than a pluralistic basis." The fault with most theories of politics from this standpoint is that they take one or the other side of the interaction process as the whole. The "individualism" of early democratic theories, for instance, assumes a certain type of human nature and neglects those forces in the environment which influence individuals. Marxism errs in the opposite direction: "It explains events and frames policies exclusively in terms of conditions provided by the environment."[9]

Dewey's revisions of democratic theory will be discussed in later chapters. It is helpful at this point to focus on his objections to Marxism, since his pluralist or interactionist position is clearest when seen in this context.

Dewey credits Marx with understanding better than anyone before him the role of economic forces in society and with showing many of capitalism's adverse effects on freedom. However, he criticizes Marxism on scientific, practical, and moral grounds. Marxism, he complains, treats the economic element as "*the* cause of *all* social change" (Dewey's emphasis). Such a theory is clearly "dated" or prescientific. Given the nature of science, the only way to know in a given instance which consequences are due to forces of economic production and which ones are not is to investigate. This means dropping any monistic theory in favor of the pluralistic position of considering "a number of interacting factors—of which a very important one is undoubtedly the economic." "There is a world-wide difference between the idea that causal sequences will be found in any given set of events taken for investigation, and the idea that *all* sets of events are linked together into a *single* whole by *one* causal law. . . . For just as *necessity* and search for a *single* all-comprehensive law was typical of the intellectual atmosphere of the forties of the last century, so *probability* and *pluralism* are the characteristics of the present state of science" (pp. 77, 84, Dewey's emphasis).

9. Dewey, "Need for Social Psychology," p. 269, and see also Mills, *Sociology and Pragmatism*, p. 428; Dewey, *Freedom and Culture*, pp. 75–76.

Dewey's practical objection to Marxist theory is that it hampers problem solving. It claims falsely for itself a comprehensive understanding of all the interconnections among social forces; from the scientific standpoint again, such knowledge is simply impossible. Consequently, Marxism is useless as a guide to political action. "Any monolithic theory of social action and social causation tends to have a ready-made answer for problems that present themselves. The wholesale character of this answer prevents critical examination and discrimination of the particular facts involved in the actual problem. In consequence, it dictates a kind of all-or-none practical activity, which in the end introduces new difficulties" (p. 100).

Nevertheless, Dewey recognizes that Marxism does offer a formula for uniting theory and practice through the notion of class struggle. But he rejects this for two main reasons. Although class conflict has helped often to bring about social change and progress, Marxism neglects the importance of cooperation as a tool for social progress and overlooks the utility of intelligence as a way of resolving class conflicts. Some method to settle social conflicts obviously must be found; but progress can be measured by the extent to which "the method of cooperative intelligence replaces the method of brute conflict." Second, the doctrine of class struggle presumes there are only class interests, a view that will not withstand a realistic examination of facts. Through cooperative inquiries and social action, men can and do discover more inclusive interests for judging their special claims.[10] Dewey counters the Marxist notion of class struggle with his notion of the democratically organized community, of which more later.

Dewey's explicit moral objections to Marxism are linked to his hostility to communism as practiced in Russia. The repressions and intolerance practiced in Russia, he believes, are rooted ultimately in Marxism's claim to be an absolute "truth." Dewey sides with those who see a practical and logical connection between philosophical and political absolutism. The arbitrariness of political power, he writes, "varies in direct ratio to the claim for absoluteness on the part of the principle in behalf of which power is exercised." Absolute principles, or more cor-

10. Dewey, *Liberalism and Social Action*, p. 81; *Freedom and Culture*, pp. 86-87.

rectly those who hold them, do not tolerate dissent; this is considered a sign of "heresy," or, in Russia, of "counterrevolution." Since someone must translate any general theory into practice, the absoluteness of the doctrine justifies the claim to absolute power. In contrast, once ideas, standards, principles, and rules are treated as experimental and tentative guides to action, they lose all "pretence of finality—the ulterior source of dogmatism."

It is no part of my purpose to evaluate the merits of Dewey's critique of Marxism. Certainly, it can be argued that he does not pay sufficient attention to the distinctions between Marx's thought and the later ideology of Marxism. Nor does he fully appreciate some of the striking similarities between his own theory and Marx's. Both Dewey and Marx break with classical liberalism on the issue of how best to interpret and evaluate political events. Central to much liberal thought is the belief that the worth of a political system can be measured by the yardstick of justice. This juridical conception of society, as it is so termed by Marx, locates the successes and failures, the value of a political community in those processes which promulgate laws, guarantee rights, and issue juridical commands. Thus, such issues as the relationship between freedom and authority, the individual and the state, obligation and disobedience—all of which are juridical in the sense that they involve contractual disputes between two or more parties—dominate liberal thought. Marx, as Allen Wood notes, self-consciously rejects juridical theory in favor of a theory of collective productive activity which treats political arrangements as epiphenomena. For Marx, a juridical interpretation of society fundamentally errs in imagining that major problems and conflicts can be remedied by legal or political processes when these processes are themselves dependent on economic forces that generate crises.[11] Although Dewey's reasons differ from Marx's, he too rejects juridical theory as formalistic. The dispute between Dewey and Marx, more than Dewey realized, is also a family quarrel.

However, Dewey is not arguing an interpretation of Marx's writings so much as he is using Marxism as a contrast to his own pluralist picture of politics. Indeed, he concludes his

11. Marx, "A Contribution To Political Economy"; also, see Wood, "The Marxian Critique of Justice."

chapter on "Totalitarian Economics and Democracy" by maintaining that an exposure of Marxism's claims to be scientific suggests as an alternative the "potential alliance between scientific method and democratic method."[12]

EXPERIMENTALISM AND DEMOCRATIC PROCEDURALISM

Dewey consistently identifies democracy with intelligence or scientific method. Both welcome a diversity of opinions before reaching any decisions, and the decisions or conclusions are open to revision in light of further experience. Dewey believes that freedom of inquiry and communication, the toleration of diverse views—these are part of both the democratic and the scientific way of life. "The very heart of political democracy is adjudication of social differences by discussion and exchange of views. This method provides a rough approximation to the method of effecting change by means of experimental inquiry and test: the scientific method. The very foundation of the democratic procedure is dependence upon experimental production of social change; and experimentation directed by working principles that are tested and developed in the very process of being tried out in action."[13]

Unlike Marxism, instrumentalism is not a theory for total transformation of the social system into the good society; it is a theory for solving problems within society in order to make specific improvements in the quality of men's lives. Problem

12. See Dewey, "Why I Am Not a Communist," pp. 135-37; *Freedom and Culture*, pp. 91, 101-2. Dewey and various other writers argue that philosophical relativism and empiricism are linked to democracy. But other theorists have argued the reverse. Totalitarianism, they maintain, is the denial of any values, and democracy is combined with a belief in the absoluteness of certain values. In contrast to both positions, Oppenheim asserts persuasively that there is no necessary logical, political, psychological, or historical connection between any one particular school of philosophy and any one political doctrine. "Relativism, Absolutism, and Democracy," pp. 951-60.

13. Dewey, "Challenge to Liberal Thought," in *Problems of Men*, p. 157. Dewey's argument is correct insofar as one accepts his definition of science as a pattern of behavior and a set of attitudes that includes tolerance, open inquiry, experimentalism, etc. But other theories of science, less methodologically oriented than Dewey's, argue that scientific activity occurs within a framework of principles and logical laws about reality that are largely arbitrary. Dewey's defense of democratic methods must and can stand on the worth of those methods apart from any appeal to scientific methodology. See Kuhn, *Structure of Scientific Revolutions*.

solving aims at transforming particular situations or remedying specific abuses. Piecemeal social reforms and incremental social change are the political equivalents of Dewey's model of trial-and-error rationalism. In an argument eleborated since by incrementalist theories of the decision-making process, Dewey admits that the piecemeal solution of problems and the openness of the democratic process may lead to some "looseness of cohesion and indefiniteness in direction of action." But, he contends, the results are likely to be more reasonable than those where men are committed to a definite creed. "There is generated a certain balance of judgment and some sort of equilibrium in social affairs. We take for granted the action of a number of diverse factors in producing any social result. There are temporary waves of insistence upon this and that particular measure and aim. But there is at least enough democracy so that in time any one tendency gets averaged up in interplay with other tendencies. An average presents qualities that are open to easy criticism. But as compared with the fanaticism generated by monistic ideas when they are put into operation, the averaging of tendencies, a movement towards a mean, is an achievement of splendor" (*Freedom and Culture*, pp. 94–95).

There are certain other parallels between Dewey's defense of democracy and incrementalist theory. Charles Lindblom's *The Intelligence of Democracy*, for example, argues that it is impossible to acquire the comprehensive knowledge necessary for central coordination of political life. Like Dewey, Lindblom emphasizes the tendency toward equilibrium in a political system open to consideration of different interests. However, these parallels must not be overstated. Experimentalism is not a politics of bargaining and compromise in the sense of Lindblom's "partisan mutual adjustment."

Some of the ways Dewey's thought differs from Lindblom's are instructive. Partisan mutual adjustment, for example, does not recognize "correct" and "incorrect" understandings of a problem. Partisans are partisans because a decision maker *"does not assume that there exists some knowable criteria acceptable to him and all the other decision makers that is sufficient, if applied, to govern adjustments among them; and he therefore does not move toward coordination by a cooperative and deliberate search for and/or application of such criteria or*

by an appeal for adjudication to those who do search and apply"
(pp. 28–29, Lindblom's emphasis). From this perspective, social
conflicts can be settled because antagonists have a common
interest in reaching agreement and are willing to adjust their
demands accordingly. Partisan mutual adjustment, Lindblom
argues, encourages agreement through bargaining, alliance
building, compromises, and persuasion rather than through
coercion. Different interests, preferences, or values are reconciled "not by sacrificing, to some degree, one or more of the
conflicting values to others, but by modifying values, interests,
or preferences, and by dropping troublesome values and formu-
lating new ones, so that agreement replaces conflict to an
important degree." For a number of reasons, he contends, this
process is likely to be more reasonable than central coordination. The multiplicity of partisans in the policy-making process
increases the probability that various aspects of a problem will
be heard. In other words, pluralism enhances the intelligence of
policy making and makes it less likely that any particular
values or interests will be overlooked. Lindblom thus locates
the reasonableness, rationality, or intelligence of this type of
political arbitration in the demands made on the partisans to
reach agreement (pp. 151, 207).

In contrast, Dewey maintains that an agreement is neither
rational nor desirable simply because it is an agreement. The
conditions which Lindblom equates with rationality—speci-
ficity of focus, adaptation to past decisions, compromise, incremental change—are simply conditions which increase the
likelihood of intelligent social action. In other words, the intelligence exemplified by scientific method is different from the
intelligence of adjustment politics. Dewey's thesis is that
"knowable criteria" exist for settling social conflicts. While
Lindblom's analysis focuses on the conflicts *between men*,
Dewey shifts attention to the experienced difficulties *in the
environment* which cause such conflicts. At the bottom of all
social conflicts is some "problem" or disharmony between men's
actions and the needs of a situation. Problems are objective;
unless this point is recognized, we miss the entire thrust of
Dewey's political writings.

Lindblom assigns a positive value to conflict as a way of
settling disputes. But as Dewey conceives the problematic in

experience, it is only a short step to the argument that the "rivalry of parties" is a "source of division and confusion," and that the first necessity for problem solving is "cooperative action" guided by "collective intelligence."[14] Thus, partisanship is dysfunctional. Consider his statement in support of the League for Independent Political Action, an organization he joined in the thirties: "We believe that actual social conditions and needs suffice to determine the direction political action should take, and we believe that this is the philosophy which underlies the democratic faith of the American people. . . . Our program is, in an ultimate sense, partial and tentative, experimental and not rigid . . . politics is a struggle for possession and use of power to settle specific issues that grow out of the country's needs and problems. . . . Because we desire a union of forces . . . we are strongly opposed to all slurs and sneers at the farmers, engineers, teachers, social workers, small merchants, clergy, newspaper people, and white-collar workers who constitute the despised middle-class."[15]

Finally, Dewey is much less optimistic than Lindblom about the reasonableness of the political process apart from cultural conditions in general. He believes that the basic freedom is freedom of mind, the education of personality. Consequently, Dewey's analysis is more reform-oriented than Lindblom's. The education of personality involves a set of demands about the organization of industry and the creation of a community where participation and power are shared widely.

As Dewey uses them, problem and science are value-laden concepts. Problems are signs of political malaise. Problem solving is not simply a method: It provides a standard for judging a society's politics. Problem solving as a central theme for political thought and as a guide to political action entails a theory of the "improving" society. By locating the knowing process in the activity whereby problematic experiences are reconstructed, pragmatism provides us with an entirely new attitude toward existing "facts." The present situation, or existing "facts," have only limited authority. That is, once experience becomes problematic, the given facts must be con-

14. Dewey, *Liberalism and Social Action*, pp. 70–71; *Freedom and Culture*, pp. 72–73.
15. Dewey, "Future of Radical Political Action," pp. 8–9.

fronted with what they exclude. In the search for a reconstructed reality where problems are solved, it is necessary to
consider the "facts" which are missing. Consider Dewey's
example of the man who is lost in the woods. He must not only
consider what is given—namely, the fact that he is lost—but he
also must consider what is needed to solve his problem, a
hypothetical map of where he started and where he must go in
order to find his way. "The lost man has no alternative except
either to wander aimlessly or else to *conceive* this inclusive
environment; and . . . this conception is just what is meant by
idea. It is not some little physical entity or piece of conscious-
ness-stuff, but is *the interpretation of the locally present
environment in reference to its absent portion,* that part to
which it is referred as another part so as give a view of a whole"
(Dewey's emphasis).[16]

Problems not only set the stage for inquiry; what one "ought"
to do becomes a function of what is needed to solve the problem.
The factual and normative are joined in the pursuit of possible
solutions to problems. Thus, Dewey avoids—indeed he rejects—the facts-values dispute that has characterized so much
social science discussion.[17] He does not give us simply a theory
of practice, of the behavior of individuals and groups; rather, he
locates theory and meaning *in* practice. Knowing and ethics are
a type of action characteristic of the man who overcomes the
contradictions and disharmonies in the world.

Dewey is quite clear that he is more concerned with explaining the nature of rational and moral conduct than he is with
spelling out exactly what the reformed society will look like
afterwards.[18] But he does argue that there are certain links
between "science" or "intelligence" and traditional liberal values.

16. Dewey, *Essays in Experimental Logic*, pp. 238-39. For an interpretation
and defense of political theory as the art of combining the possible and the
desirable, see Spitz, "Politics and Critical Imagination," pp. 419-35.
17. I have discussed the implications of Dewey's pragmatism for the study
of politics in Damico, "Analysis and Advocacy."
18. "The art of which our times needs in order to create a new type of
individuality is the art which, being sensitive to the technology and science that
are the moving forces of our time, will envisage the expansive, the social,
culture which they may be made to serve. I am not anxious to depict the form
which this emergent individualism will assume. Indeed, I do not see how it can
be described until more progress has been made in its production" (Dewey,
Individualism, p. 99).

This is evident when he discusses the similarity between the methods of democracy and the methods of science. But there is more to it than this. Dewey takes seriously the traditional classical belief that the quality of a country's politics depends on the civic virtue of its people. Referring to the use of intelligence in physical inquiry, Dewey writes: "Suppose that what now happens in limited circles were extended and generalized. Would the outcome be oppression or emancipation? Inquiry is a challenge, not a passive conformity; application is a means of growth, not of repression. The general adoption of the scientific attitude in human affairs would mean nothing less than a revolutionary change in morals, religion, politics and industry.... Take science . . . for what it is, and we shall begin to envisage it as a potential creator of new values and ends. We shall have an intimation, on a wide and generous scale, of the release, the increased initiative, independence and inventiveness, which science now brings in its own specialized fields to the individual scientist. It will be seen as a means of originality and individual variation" (*Individualism*, pp. 155, 160–61). Dewey thus argues that the commitment to intelligence would serve as the harbinger of a major cultural transformation. Although we shall see serious difficulties with Dewey's analysis of politics, one of his major achievements is to make clear why political activism, not political quietism, is the only course open to men committed to improving the quality of social life. As one writer remarks, "it is a mistake to complain that the progressives sought to institutionalize a mood without recognizing that this was also their most characteristic achievement."[19]

As presented so far, there are three major weaknesses in Dewey's account of politics: his conception of the problematic, his overestimation of the benefits to be gained by focusing on the specific, and his underestimation of the requirements for organized political action. Dewey wrote an essay for *The New Republic* with the revealing title "Education as Politics." In discussing the need for an education that develops a critical intelligence among students, he asserts: "When this happens schools will be the dangerous outposts of a humane civilization but they will also begin to be supremely interesting places. For

19. Welter, *Popular Education and Democratic Thought*, p. 266.

it will then have come about that *education and politics are one and the same thing because politics will have to be in fact what it now pretends to be, the intelligent management of social affairs"* (emphasis added). Reversing the title of Dewey's essay provides an insight into his political theory. Politics as education, not merely educational, is a doctrine that comes very close to explaining all political life in terms of the need for more "inquiry." Dewey often imagines that more facts, further investigation, and increased knowledge will settle social conflicts in "the interests of all—or at least of the great majority." Central to such argument is the notion that social problems are "objective" in the same way problems in nature are; reason, therefore, can manage the former in the same clear-cut manner that it does the latter. "'Laws' of social life, when it is genuinely human," says Dewey, "are like laws of engineering. If you want certain results, certain means must be found and employed."[20]

Dewey's arguments on these points are unconvincing. He describes problems as though they involve only a conflict between a "correct," that is a "scientific," and a nonscientific understanding of a situation. We have noted Dewey's criticism of the Marxist doctrine that intensification of the class conflict is the way to solve that conflict. But his proposed alternative is far from adequate: "What generates violent strife is failure to bring the conflict into the light of intelligence where the conflicting interests can be adjudicated in behalf of the interest of the great majority" (*Liberalism and Social Action*, p. 80).

Dewey fails to consider seriously Marx's contention that different classes want different things not because of misunderstanding or perversity but because the economic structure is such that their interests are antithetical. One group wants to maintain certain institutional arrangements; the other wants to bring about a new pattern of relationships. It is not simply a question of understanding versus misunderstanding; rather, men's activities and consequently their interests differ because they occupy different places in the economic structure of society.[21] Whether it is a dispute between workers and employers, a conflict occasioned by religious or racial intolerance, or a

20. Dewey, "Education as Politics," in *Characters and Events*, 2:781: *Liberalism and Social Action*, p. 79; *Public and Its Problems*, p. 197.
21. Compare Mills, *Sociology and Pragmatism*, pp. 412-13.

dispute between conservationists and land developers or industrialists, it is evident that their interests are not capable of total reconciliation. Despite the currency of the notion that communication is the path out of social troubles, there are good reasons for suspecting that the balance of power among partisans has more to do with the outcome of most social conflicts than does reason.

Dewey's difficulty is that he believes all problems can be reduced to some difficulty in man's interaction with the "objective" environment. This obscures the fact that some conflicts and problematic situations involve rival claims among men. Those in power often deny that the situation is problematic, that conditions need changing. This is a conflict of values and interests, not a difficulty in man's interaction with the environment. Therefore, Dewey's suggestion that conflicts be settled by postponing a decision until partisans have agreed on the "needs" of a situation is no solution.

Dewey does reform our thinking about political creeds by arguing persuasively that their "truth" often hinges upon their ability to state their doctrines so they can be neither proved nor disproved by what occurs in the real world. But one of the oldest and perhaps the most common errors in philosophy is the tendency for a man who has uncovered some weakness in previous philosophies to fall into the trap of exaggerating the merits of an opposing principle or method. Dewey is guilty of something like this in emphasizing the merits of reducing intellectual inquiry to the question of specific cases. The fact that men disagree over general and abstract creeds does not justify the conclusion that they are less likely to disagree sharply about specific issues. Indeed, it is precisely the application of general principles to specific cases which fosters some of the most bitter disputes and antagonisms among men. For example, men committed to the principle of equal educational opportunities may divide strongly when it comes to the question of how to guarantee those opportunities. An appeal to the general principle may play some part in adjusting their differences. When a conflict is not over the "needs of a situation" but over the meaning and implications of various values, beliefs, and interests, the conflict cannot be settled by attempting to transfer the difficulty to some other realm.

Dewey's belief that the "ultimate fate is the fatality of ignorance, and the ultimate wickedness is lack of faith in the possibilities of intelligence applied inventively and constructively" accounts for his aversion to ideological groups, parties, or movements which "embody moral emotions rather than the insight and the policy of intelligence." This also explains why Dewey never identified completely with any party, although he supported many liberal causes. He campaigned actively for the election of Norman Thomas, but he did so as a member of the Intercollegiate Socialist Society, an adjunct of the Socialist Party composed mainly of intellectuals organized as a study group. Similarly, Dewey avoids calling any of his political proposals socialism, even his argument for the public control of industry: Socialism is too much a "party word." The crux of Dewey's style of politics is this effort to shift attention from the antagonisms among different groups and classes to their common stake in solving "problems." Consequently, no conventional political labels can be affixed to Dewey or to his theory of political activism. "This," Sidney Hook argues, "is what we should expect about anyone faithful to the spirit of the experimental philosophy."[22]

Since the intellectual growth of the individual is pivotal to all Dewey's philosophical theories, it is not surprising that he condemns much of the normal game of politics. He actually expresses two somewhat different attitudes toward the characteristic features of electoral politics. In his early writings, he argues that parties and elections are little more than sham. "It would be a waste of words to expatiate on the meaninglessness of present political platforms, parties and issues. The old-time slogans are still reiterated, and to a few these words still seem to have a real meaning. But it is too evident to need argument that on the whole our politics, as far as they are not covertly manipulated in behalf of the pecuniary advantage of groups, are in a state of confusion, issues are improvised from week to week with a constant shift of allegiance. . . . Political apathy broken by recurrent sensations and spasms is the natural outcome" (*Individualism*, pp. 59-60). In *Freedom and Culture*,

22. Dewey, "Social Psychology and Social Progress," in *Characters and Events*, 2:719; for Dewey's relationship to the Socialist party in America, see Shannon, *Socialist Party of America*, pp. 54-56; Hook, *John Dewey*, p. 162.

he considers more carefully the significance of parties and elections and the way they affect the exercise of power. Free discussion, social pluralism, voluntary associations—these democratic procedures increase the probability of trial-and-error political action. Dewey's expanded attitude is influenced by his belief that in 1939 a new set of circumstances had arisen. Conditions in totalitarian countries, he argues, demonstrate a large gulf between a country having suffrage and popular representation and a country without them. Although still insisting that democracy is more than a form of government, he now holds that electoral politics has a value "critics of partial democracy [including himself] have not realized" (pp. 93–94).

However, a clear ambivalence remains in Dewey's judgment of political activity when compared to experimentalism and science as modes of activity. "What purports to be experiment in the social field is very different from experiment in natural science; it is rather a process of trial-and-error accompanied with some degree of hope and a great deal of talk. Legislation is a matter of more or less intelligent improvisation aiming at palliating conditions by means of patchwork policies . . . the real problem is that of building up an intelligent and capable civil-service" (*Freedom and Culture*, p. 65). Dewey never balances satisfactorily his desire to promote an activist political philosophy that expands the scientific management of social affairs with his recognition that political activity is not like scientific activity. In effect, he does not recognize the problems peculiar to political action. His standards of rational conduct make him suspicious of parties and political movements for these often depend for their success on loyalties created by uncritical faith in the group's program or its general principles. But it is difficult to imagine how any political group could motivate its members by insisting upon its own limitations and the merits of the opposition.

Dewey underestimates also the positive functions of social conflict. Competition between parties, groups, and different philosophies is not simply a necessary evil but a positive good. It provides some modest insurance that various grievances will be heard. Even though electoral politics must compromise principles with a "great deal of talk," it nevertheless helps to prevent political power from being exercised arbitrarily. In praising politics for what it could be, Dewey mistakenly criticizes much of what it is.[23] This is characteristic of many progressives who proposed to improve political life by taking the politics "out" of government.

Dewey's criticisms and rejection of partisan politics are a weakness noted often in his theory. But implicit in such criticisms is a compliment; ignoring a writer is a harsher, more unremitting judgment. C. Wright Mills, one of pragmatism's most important critics, obviously shares Dewey's belief that men must engage in those forms of social *praxis* which can liberate each individual to be an actor rather than a spectator, a free man rather than a victim. It is easy to recognize pragmatist themes in Mills' own work. Consider his claim that it is the task of the sociological imagination "to grasp history and biography and the relations between the two within society . . . to translate personal troubles into public issues, and public issues into the terms of their human meaning for a variety of individuals." Mills' own writings evidence his concern "to help the individual become a self-educating man" and "to combat those forces which are destroying genuine publics."[24]

Mills' sympathy for Dewey's attempt to unite theory and practice and analysis and advocacy explains the intensity of his quarrel with pragmatism. Mills' major objection is that Dewey never grasps fully, or understands, how the particular structure of a society distributes power. Whenever opposing groups confront each other because of the structural antagonisms of society, what "we get from Dewey is not a choice supporting one or the other." Rather, Mills continues, what we get is "the plea that when social science develops like physical science, we can solve or obviate such problems."[25] It is also clear that Mills has Dewey in mind when he complains that "liberal practicality" tends either to be "a-political" or to explain political

23. One of the best statements of the value of politics because of its compromises, its preoccupation with procedures and forms, and its conflict of interests is Crick, In Defence of Politics.

24. Mills, Sociological Imagination, pp. 6, 186-87. For a further discussion of the pragmatist themes evident in Mills' writings, see the introduction by Horowitz in Mills, Sociology and Pragmatism, pp. 11-31. A nice summary of the criticisms of Dewey's work from a Marxist perspective is given by Bernstein, Praxis and Action, pp. 227-29.

25. Mills, Sociology and Pragmatism, p. 405.

conflicts in terms of such pathological features as the "anti-social" or "corruption." In short, Dewey's political activism is not radical enough; pragmatism's concepts of method, intelligence, and "problematization" postpone a fuller recognition of the political problem.[26]

Mills is essentially correct in arguing that Dewey's pragmatism is not sufficiently "political." But this judgment leaves untouched still some of the more critical and characteristic features of Dewey's instrumentalism and naturalism. Dewey's system of thought unites analysis and advocacy. For Dewey, the activity of critical inquiry is not morally or politically neutral. Just as his account of knowing and ethics entails an activist attitude toward experience, his analysis of critical inquiry is socially loaded. The norms of critical inquiry point to the need for a reconstructed liberal theory and a reconstructed democratic society.

26. Mills, *Sociological Imagination*, p. 88; *Sociology and Pragmatism*, pp. 382, 423.

5. The New Liberalism

$\mathbf{T}$OWARD THE END of the nineteenth century and in the early part of the twentieth century, writers in both England and America began to use such phrases as "authentic democracy," the "new freedom," and the "new liberalism" to indicate that old doctrines needed updating. In America, these ideas were related to the emergence of progressivism. Political activists and philosophers alike began to demand that ideas come to grips with reality. The demand that more attention be paid to the substance than to the form of politics, law, and economics was usually made in the language of pragmatism, the philosophical lodestone of this period. Individual freedom and the democratic state remain pre-eminent values, but the "old" liberalism's views of how best to realize these values are sharply criticized. In part, the new liberalism is simply an effort to devise new means for achieving traditional liberal ends. "The ends remain valid," says Dewey. "But the means of attaining them demand a radical change in economic institutions and the political arrangements based upon them."[1] There is also the suggestion that the substance of liberalism must be defined anew. It is not

1. Cf. Forcey, *Crossroads of Liberalism*, p. x; the best study of the "revolt against formalism" during this period is White, *Social Thought*; Dewey, "Liberty and Social Control," in *Problems of Men*, p. 125.

surprising to find Dewey referring to two liberalisms, the old and the new. This chapter first sketches some of the major distinctions between earlier and later formulations of liberalism, then looks at Dewey's discussion of these distinctions. Second, Dewey's idea of freedom, the core of his version of the new liberalism, is evaluated.

MODERNIZING LIBERALISM

Classical liberalism is the liberalism of constitutionalism (John Locke), the negative state and individualism (John Stuart Mill), and, in political economy, laissez-faire (Adam Smith).[2] Although there are important differences among these early advocates of liberalism, each sees the major political problem as equipping the government with sufficient powers to arbitrate conflicts which threaten the social order, and at the same time guarding against the excesses and tyranny of governmental power. Since liberalism originated at a time when arbitrary government was the most obvious restraint on freedom, suspicion of governmental power is a major feature of classical liberalism. To the liberal, such power is to be used only when the need is great and not met otherwise. The French writer Morellet expressed the general view in this terse statement: "Since liberty is a natural state, and restrictions are, on the contrary, the state of compulsion, by giving back liberty everything reassumes its own place, and everything is in peace, provided only that thieves and murderers continue to be caught."[3]

Whether defined as the enjoyment of natural rights or as the absence of restraints, freedom is seen as depending on a system of mutual forbearance: As long as he does not interfere with others, a man can enjoy his liberty. John Stuart Mill's famous essay "On Liberty" best exemplifies the effort to distinguish between those actions which primarily concern the individual and those actions which are injurious to the interests of others.

2. These are only the more obvious names associated with classical liberalism. I make no assumption that this sketch captures the complexity of a theory which contains many intellectual streams. But there is some utility in drawing the larger distinctions between the two liberalisms.

3. Morellet, *Lettres de l'Abbé à Lord Shelburne,* p. 102, quoted in Halévy, *Growth of Philosophic Radicalism,* p. 116.

Whether or not Mill's principles really enable us to distinguish between private and public acts is not important at this point. What is significant is his insistence that resort to social or political control should be rare. Even when governmental actions do not infringe on liberty, Mill advances a number of reasons for being wary of governmental interference. He approves of the political economists' arguments that the "ordinary processes of industry" are best left alone. And he advises that although the government could possibly do something better than men acting separately, it is wiser to let them do it themselves "as means to their own mental education." Finally, he emphasizes that any addition to the government's power is an evil to be avoided.[4] The doctrine of the negative state was reinforced strongly by the expectation that the free market system would enable each individual to become whatever his talents and tastes dictated. In teaching that each individual who pursues his own interests also serves the happiness of the greatest number, Adam Smith provides a further defense against state interference.[5]

In contrast to the early liberals, the new liberals are united in the belief that many problems do require the use of public—that is, state—power to solve them. Whether we look at such English writers as T. H. Green[6] and Leonard Hobhouse or John Dewey in America, positive action by the state is no longer viewed as the exception. Left alone, man is unable to make his way in the world. When freedom from state power passes through the economic system, it translates too easily into freedom for a few and economic bondage for the many. With the rise of large

4. Mill, *Utilitarianism, Liberty, and Representative Government*, pp. 203–23. An entire literature has grown up around the value and usefulness of Mill's theory of liberty. A sharp criticism of Mill's work and of liberalism in general is Wolff's *Poverty of Liberalism*. A balanced defense of Mill's essay is presented by Benn and Peters, *Principles of Political Thought*, pp. 257–71.

5. The links between Smith's economic theories and the political theories of the utilitarians and the early liberals is examined exhaustively by Halévy, *Growth of Philosophic Radicalism*, particularly pp. 88–120.

6. A special word of caution, however, regarding Green's views toward state activity: Although his definition of freedom as a form of self-perfection leads him to assign the state a positive role in promoting conditions favorable to moral development, Richter cautions that when Green was faced with choosing between socialism or having the state establish only minimum standards of economic well-being, "his choice was minimum standards" (*The Politics of Conscience*, p. 285).

corporations and the concentration of capital in a few hands, those already advantaged by the workings of the economic system benefit the most from the absence of governmental interference. Dewey is forceful on this point. "The notion that men are equally free to act if only the same legal arrangements apply equally to all—irrespective of differences in education, in command of capital, and the control of the social environment which is furnished by the institution of property—is a pure absurdity, as facts have demonstrated." Therefore, the new liberals can argue that the use of governmental power to regulate working conditions or to promote a wider distribution of wealth actually enlarges the sphere of freedom for most men. "The restraint of the aggressor is the freedom of the sufferer."[7]

The belief that mutual aid, not merely mutual forbearance, marks the good society is crucial to the new liberalism. To make liberalism a more reform-oriented political theory, its proponents attack the individualism of classical liberalism from a number of perspectives. And no one has done this more persuasively than has Dewey.

Throughout the 1930s, Dewey examined continuously the problem of individuality and collective action. He was writing in an atmosphere where the doctrines of laissez-faire liberalism seemed responsible for the misery wrought by the depression and for the state's initial reluctance to attack economic problems. *Individualism Old and New*, and *Liberalism and Social Action*, plus a collection of essays published later as *Problems of Men*, have as their common topic the growing corporateness in America and the consequent need for collective action to solve problems. Dewey's major thesis is that "individualistic liberalism" sets up a false antagonism between the individual and organized society, but that "collectivistic liberalism" does away with this opposition.

Before revising the doctrine of individualism, Dewey admits it did perform several important tasks at the time it originated. Once men began to champion individual rights, older forms of

7. Dewey, "Philosophies of Freedom," in *On Experience, Nature, and Freedom*, p. 271; Hobhouse, *Liberalism*, p. 50. Hobhouse also states that "in general, we are justified in regarding the State as one among many forms of human association for the maintenance and improvement of life." And this, he continues, "is the point at which we stand furthest from the older liberalism" (see p. 71).

organized power, especially the state, were exposed as arbitrary and oppressive. Individualism also taught that freedom of discussion and of expression were important for man's growth. But the tragedy of liberalism, Dewey contends, has been its lack of a historical sense. It has been slow to adjust to changing conditions. In short, liberalism itself has become a formal and fixed creed.

Failure to see that the practical significance of means and ends varies with historical circumstances has caused a split among liberals. Many now support governmental action to improve the condition of the economically disadvantaged to make them free in fact as well as in theory. But Dewey observes that others use liberal principles of "rugged individualism" to defend illiberal ends. For example, the Liberty League of the thirties and the libertarians of the seventies claim title to the tradition of liberalism by insisting that any governmental action infringes on liberty. Such a claim, Dewey argues, is spurious. Laissez-faire political and economic principles no longer advance political freedom. And it is no sign of political virtue to keep faith with the form of a tradition at the expense of its substance. Much of Dewey's critique of the old liberalism pivots on revising its form to give practical effect to its values.

From his writings, we can identify three features of liberalism which Dewey believed needed to be reminted in modern coin: its conception of human nature, its presumption of a permanent opposition between the individual and organized social action or between freedom and authority, and its laissez-faire principles of political economy.

The "essential fallacy of classic Liberalism" is that it provides no theory of man's development through society. Rather, men are cloaked in the mantle of natural rights, powers, and liberties as though these were "ready-made possessions" apart from what happens to men in society.[8] But men, Dewey remonstrates

8. T. H. Green makes almost the same complaint against the early liberal writers. They leave "out of sight the process by which men have been clothed with rights and duties, and with senses of right and duty, which are neither natural nor derived from a sovereign power." Dewey was quite familiar with Green's work and wrote three early essays about his philosophy. But Dewey was interested primarily in Green's criticisms of British empiricism, not in his political writings. See Green, *Lectures on Principles of Political Obligation*, p. 121.

constantly, are always social beings. "Individuality in a social and moral sense is something to be wrought out. It means initiative, inventiveness, varied resourcefulness, assumption of responsibility in choice of belief and conduct. These are not gifts, but achievements. As achievements, they are not absolute but relative to the use that is to be made of them. And this use varies with the environment" (*Reconstruction*, p. 194). Dewey's writings often give the impression that the good life is easy to achieve, that all that is needed is a greater reliance on science. But his argument here is exactly the opposite. Dewey is challenging the assumption of early liberalism that removal of external restrictions and formal obstacles is all that is necessary to further individualism. This theory is too easy. It imagines that the task of political action is largely negative—setting up No Trespass signs around "natural rights." But if individuality is something to be won, then the task of politics is infinitely more varied and difficult: the creation of a positive pattern of interactions between individual and environment. In "The Future of Liberalism," Dewey writes: "Liberalism knows that social conditions may restrict, distort and almost prevent the development of individuality. It therefore takes an active interest in the working of social institutions that have a bearing, positive or negative, upon the growth of individuals who shall be rugged in fact and not merely in abstract theory. It is as much interested in the positive construction of favorable institutions, legal, political and economic, as it is in the work of removing abuses and overt oppressions."[9]

One of the first major revisions of liberalism occurred with publication of Mill's essay "On Liberty." In recognizing that political institutions are part of a larger social setting, Mill argued that it was necessary to defend individual freedom not simply against an arbitrary government but against intolerant public opinion. The enjoyment of liberty was no longer merely a function of constitutional government; it also depended on a liberal society. Liberalism was revised further with recognition that governmental power could restrain factory owners, regulate working conditions, and combat monopolies in order to release the workingman from the restraints of private power. These revisions do not necessarily alter the dichotomy between

9. Dewey, "Future of Liberalism," in *Problems of Men*, p. 136.

the individual and society established by classical liberalism. The evolution of liberalism still reflects a society where individuals on one side confront various coercive social institutions on the other. Mill, for instance, carries over the liberal suspicion of political institutions and applies it to society. But Dewey's revisions are more extensive. He argues against both the individual-society dichotomy and such a negative view of organized social power.[10]

Individuality and community are two sides of a single phenomenon. Since men live in association, the individual's opportunities for action, initiative, and choice become a function of his participation in a community which uses its collective resources to promote the good of each member. This was evident in America's pioneer period, but the connection has been little understood. "The true individualism of that era has been eclipsed because it has been misunderstood. It is not often treated as if it were an exaltation of individuals free from social relations and responsibilities. Marsh expresses its genuine spirit when he refers, as he does constantly, to the *community* of individuals. The essence of our earlier pioneer individualism was not non-social, much less anti-social; it involved no indifference to the claims of society. Its working ideal was neighborliness and mutual service. . . . Community relationships were to enable an individual to reach a fuller manifestation of his own powers, and this development was in turn to be a factor in modifying the organized and stated civil and political order so that more individuals would be capable of genuine participation in the self-government and self-movement of society" (Dewey's emphasis).[11] Most men will respond to this vision of a "community of individuals." But a vision is no substitute for a set of propositions which indicate how the ideal can bring pressure to bear on the real. Socialism and, in a much wider context, participation are key aspects of Dewey's program for translating his theory into a more perfect practice.

Liberalism and the economic doctrine of laissez-faire are often equated. This equation has created considerable con-

10. Compare Sabine, *History of Political Theory*, p. 710; Dewey, *Individualism*, pp. 33-34.
11. Dewey, "James Marsh and American Philosophy," in *Problems of Men*, pp. 374-75.

fusion. Advocates of laissez-faire view capitalism as a system of voluntary contracts guaranteeing that men's economic acts and their other acts and choices will be free. Critics of laissez-faire deny that most contracts in a capitalist economy are voluntary. They argue that the imbalance of power between the individual actor and corporate actors, and between workers and capitalists, leads to a situation where most men lack resources or opportunities to live a free life. And each side claims to be defending liberalism.[12]

Whether or not there is any necessary connection between liberalism and a particular economic order is still debated widely. Dewey insists that a connection exists. Liberal values, he argues, can be realized only in a socialist economy. For Dewey, liberalism is a theory which defines the good society as one where each individual is self-directing. To be liberal means to value each man's right to choose and to act according to his own judgment. Only socialism provides man with resources and opportunities for living a life in conformity with his own nature and rational choices.

A recent work by James Coleman can help introduce Dewey's discussion of socialism. Coleman argues that in order to understand the power and structure of modern societies, it is necessary to note the differences between natural persons and juristic persons. Natural persons are physical persons of the sort we all are; juristic persons are intangible entities which literally cannot be seen. Juristic persons include corporations and other entities which act through agents. In other words, two parallel structures of relationships coexist in society: the pattern of relationships among natural persons, and the pattern of relationships among juristic persons which employ and use natural persons as resources. Coleman's major thesis is that as the power of juristic actors has increased, the power of natural persons has decreased correspondingly. Corporate bodies, for example, have greater control over information and thus are more likely to dominate any exchange between themselves and natural persons; corporate actors favor other corporate actors

12. For a sophisticated defense and a criticism of the identification of liberalism and the free market, see, respectively, Hayek, *Road to Serfdom*, and Macpherson, *Democratic Theory*. I am persuaded by Sartori's argument that liberalism existed before laissez-faire and can exist beyond it. *See Democratic Theory*, pp. 364-67.

in making decisions and in providing services. In practice, this means "a peculiar bias in the direction that social and economic activities take."[13] Those interests which have been collected successfully to create juristic persons are those likely to prevail in society. The individual is often right in feeling that he is a mere pawn in a game dominated by others.

Dewey views socialism partly as a method for controlling the abuses of economic power in order to enlarge the freedom of natural persons. Just as early liberals recognized that uncontrolled political power leads to abuse of the ruled by the rulers, so the new liberals recognize that uncontrolled economic power leads to abuse of the many by the few. The early liberals "had no glimpse of the fact that private control of the new forces of production, forces which affect the life of everyone, would operate in the same way as private unchecked control of political power. They saw the need for new legal institutions, and of different political conditions as a means to political liberty. But they failed to perceive that social control of economic forces is equally necessary if anything approaching economic equality and liberty is to be realized" (*Liberalism and Social Action*, p. 36).

Individuality and liberty depend on the conditions in which individuals find themselves, and social policies must be altered accordingly. Dewey reviews the economic inequalities and poverty in America during the 1930s and finds "No doubt in my own mind that *laissez-faire* liberalism is played out, largely because of the fruits of its own policies. Any system that cannot provide elementary security for millions has no claim to the title of being organized in behalf of liberty and the development of individuals."[14]

Dewey's advocacy of socialism does not include much discussion of how to redistribute power. He does speak of the need for the "cooperative control of industry," and he does urge creation of a council composed of the "captains of industry and finance" and representatives of labor and of government. But he explains neither how these men are to be chosen nor what should be their respective powers and the powers of the council.[15] Dewey

---

13. Coleman, *Power and the Structure of Society*, p. 49.
14. Dewey, "Future of Liberalism," in *Problems of Men*, p. 132.
15. Dewey says nothing, for instance, about the wage relationship. His lack

is less interested in how the control of the forces of production itself would work than he is with the educational impact of such control. Socialism is a method for collectively controlling economic forces; even more important, it is an ethical ideal—a political and economic means to the development of individuality through practice. Dewey is concerned with the activity of the natural person. Opportunities, choices, and actions are limited increasingly by forces beyond individual control. "The theory of the self-actuated and self-governing individual receives a rude shock when massed activity has a potency which individual effort can no longer claim" (*Freedom and Culture,* p. 63).

Although Dewey is sensitive to the hardships imposed by unemployment, poor wages, and unsafe working conditions, he argues that the economic problem cannot be thought of simply as a "bread-and-butter" issue. The deeper issue is the type of society men are going to form. From this moral standpoint, he criticizes capitalism. "This state of affairs must exist so far as society is organized on a basis of division between laboring classes and leisure classes. The intelligence of those who do things becomes hard in the unremitting struggle with things; that of those freed from the discipline of occupation becomes luxurious and effeminate. Moreover, the majority of human beings still lack economic freedom. Their pursuits are fixed by accident and necessity of circumstance; they are not the normal expression of their own powers interacting with the needs and resources of the environment. Our economic conditions still relegate many men to a servile status. As a consequence, the intelligence of those in control of the practical situation is not liberal. Instead of playing freely upon the subjugation of the world for human ends, it is devoted to the manipulation of other men for ends that are non-human in so far as they are exclusive" (*Democracy and Education,* p. 136).

Socialism—mass participation in the factory and in controlling the consequences of the economic system—is Dewey's solution for the "crisis in culture," i.e., the gap between the ideal

---

of a theory of socialism as an economic system accounts for the superficiality of those writers who have tried to rely solely on him for such a theory. Two studies which rarely go beyond making an impassioned plea for the good life are Nathanson, *John Dewey,* and Steibel, "John Dewey's Philosophy of Democracy."

of a community of individuals and the reality of the private and self-serving control of industry. Enactment of social legislation in a welfare state may be beneficial, but it is not enough. There must be a new "social orientation and organization," including socialization of production, to permit the economic structure itself to pivot on the needs of the population (*Individualism*, p. 135). This is identical with the "recovery of composed, effective and creative individuality." Socialism, then, is a further route to a community that uses "socially organized intelligence" to solve its problems.

If labels are needed, Dewey's political creed comes very close to democratic socialism. Many of the problems with interpretation and evaluation of Dewey's work, therefore, have to do with his political technology, his account of how to get from where we are to where we need to be in order to solve our problems. Such difficulties become apparent when we look closer at Dewey's efforts to modernize liberalism so that it can serve as a guide to a comprehensive program of political action.

While most observers view Roosevelt's New Deal as the triumph of political pragmatism in America, Dewey did not uncritically celebrate it. Many of his political writings in the 1930s criticize the government for improvising programs to meet "special occasions" and for a lack of general guidelines. Specific problem solving is not enough. The strength of classical liberalism, he asserts, stemmed from "a thought out social philosophy, a theory of politics sufficiently definite and coherent to be easily translated into a program of policies to be pursued." The new liberalism also must construct a political philosophy with room for "far reaching experiments in construction of a new social order."[16]

Dewey's arguments here have led to the charge that there is a basic inconsistency within his work: "Comprehensive measures, however, are in fact in direct contravention to the spirit

16. Hartz, *Liberal Tradition*; Dewey, *Individualism*, pp. 114-15. Nevertheless, Dewey remains suspicious of "wholesale creeds." In this same work which calls for a new liberal creed, he writes: "We are given to thinking of society in large and vague ways. We should forget 'society' and think of law, industry, religion, medicine, politics, art, education, philosophy—and think of them in the plural. For points of contact are not the same for any two persons and hence the questions which the interests and occupations pose are never twice the same" (*Individualism*, p. 166).

of trial-and-error procedure, which implies cautious, well-thought-out, and manageable experiments so that the harm done by any errors may not be irremedial. . . . Consequently, Dewey's advocacy of positive measures is invariably carried to the extent where these measures come in direct conflict with his laboriously argued out philosophy of trial-and-error."[17] There is much that one can sympathize with in this criticism by Somjee. The major thrust of Dewey's philosophy is toward political action that remedies specific evils. And certainly Dewey's constant attacks on general principles, or "inclusive ideals," do discourage efforts to link various reform policies under one political umbrella or social program. But it can be argued in his defense that nothing in his philosophy *prohibits* support for a comprehensive social program. Although he has always insisted that understanding must start with specific experiences, by the 1930s he argues that experience has revealed an interdependency among such problems as unemployment, unsafe working conditions, the insignificance of the individual's participation in directing the purposes of his work, and the principles of capitalism. Consequently, these specific problems can be solved fully only by changing the economic system itself.

Dewey attempts to resolve the tension created by his admiration for the piecemeal and trial-and-error methods of science and his desire that comprehensive changes in social conditions be made by distinguishing between a broad vision and its incremental implementation. Liberalism must become "radical" in the sense of bringing about thoroughgoing changes in institutions; but since the goal is creation of a new type of man and a new type of society, the process will be gradual and will require changes on many fronts. "The human *ideal* is indeed comprehensive. As a standpoint from which to view existing conditions and judge the direction change should take, it cannot be too inclusive. But the problem of production of change is one of infinite attention to means; and means can be determined only by definite analysis of the conditions of each problem as it presents itself" (Dewey's emphasis).[18]

17. Somjee, *Political Theory of John Dewey*, p. 156.
18. Dewey, *Freedom and Culture*, p. 170. In "Economic Basis of the New Society," Dewey makes this distinction: "An immense difference divides the *planned* society from a *continuously planning* society. The former requires fixed blueprints imposed from above and therefore involving reliance upon physical

Despite Dewey's awareness of the utility of a cohesive social and political program, it is true, nevertheless, that the final impact of his arguments is to discourage the type of thought and inquiry necessary to develop such a program. Dewey agrees that a sound political creed must organize the discrete and the concrete into a generalized system of principles for interpreting and evaluating specific political phenomena. But he fails to recognize that such a program will not be born of a "scientific" mode of inquiry which insists on the uniqueness of each experience and always focuses on concrete and specific problems. Although Dewey does not want to restrict the range of political discourse and inquiry, the practical effect of his writings is to encourage the adjustment style of politics, for which he criticizes the New Deal.

Dewey's dilemma stems from his mistrust of creeds—these too easily become dogmatic and formal—and his perception, however incomplete, of the need for such creeds. This is the major obstacle to his effort to modernize liberalism. "As a social philosophy, 'liberalism' runs the gamut of which a vague temper of mind—often called forward-looking—is one extreme, and a definite creed as to the purposes and methods of social action is another. The first is too vague to afford any steady guide in conduct; the second is so specific and fixed as to result in dogma, and thus to end in an illiberal mind. Liberalism as a method of intelligence, prior to being a method of action, as a method of experimentation based on insight into both social desires and actual conditions, escapes the dilemma. It signifies the adoption of the scientific habit of mind in application to social affairs."[19]

But liberalism as "intelligence" does not really escape the dilemma posed by Dewey. For instance, if we ask how socialism as an element of a new liberalism is to come about, Dewey answers that there must be a greater reliance on intelligence in social affairs. He argues in *Individualism Old and New*, for instance, that once men "recognize" the corporate age in which they live, "the issue will define itself" as the public control of

and psychological force to secure conformity to them. The latter means the release of intelligence through the widest form of cooperative give-and-take" (*Intelligence*, pp. 431–32).

19. "Oliver Wendell Holmes," in *Characters and Events*, 1:100–101.

industry. In other words, Dewey wants to reform political life by reforming men's ideas and beliefs. Politics *as* politics is played down. "Politics is a means, not an end." Dewey sharply criticizes the exigencies of organized politics with its slogans and its preoccupation with immediate demands.

The spread of intelligence "does not demand the creation of a formal organization; it does demand that a sense of the need and opportunity should possess a sufficiently large number of minds" (*Individualism*, p. 139). But Dewey must explain how or why "recognition" is going to overcome the reluctance of the capitalist class to give up its position in the economic system. The new individualism would have society use its collective resources and socially organized intelligence to further the growth of each person. However, "The greatest obstacle to that vision is, I repeat, the perpetuation of the older individualism now reduced, as I have said, to the utilization of science and technology for ends of private pecuniary gain. I sometimes wonder if those who are conscious of present ills but who direct their blows of criticism at everything except this obstacle are not stirred by motives which they unconsciously prefer to keep below consciousness" (pp. 99–100). Dewey almost recognizes here the chief defect in his confidence that the power of reason can change social and economic arrangements. What he does not see is that the inability of intelligence to overcome refractory social habits and beliefs which are closely tied to men's interests is the broken link in his whole chain of reasoning.

Five years later, Dewey realized that, in order to be effective, intelligence must be backed by the power of organized individuals. "It is in organization for action that liberals are weak," he writes in *Liberalism and Social Action*, "and without this organization there is danger that democratic ideals may go by default." But it is still the political highroad that Dewey chooses to travel. In the same work, he regards electioneering as "propaganda" and as the manipulation of symbols. Thus, an appeal to all liberals to unite behind the general goal of socializing the forces of production is as far as he is willing to go in meeting the need for a "concrete program of action" (p. 91). But such a broadly defined goal and an acknowledged hostility toward party politics provides Dewey with slim basis for hope or confidence.

THE IDEA OF FREEDOM

Criticisms of Dewey's political technology must not blind us to the fact that it is part of a new democratic ontology. Pragmatist political philosophy has been so highly touted for its "practical" qualities that it is easy to ignore the rationalist assumptions on which it rests, the most important being that politics can become more like education. Education is never simply a method for Dewey; it is a way of life enabling each man to have the powers and opportunities to develop his capacities in harmony with the rest of society. A renascent liberalism requires more than the discovery of new means to old ends. Rather, there must be a basic alteration in the ideas of freedom and individuality that define the liberal experience. One of the major obstacles, according to Dewey, to a liberalism relevant to modern conditions is an outdated conception of freedom which, primarily negative and individualistic in its emphasis, discourages positive and collective social action aimed at solving widespread problems. Again, Dewey's theme is that performance counts: "Consequences in the lives of individuals are the criterion and measure of policy and judgment" (*Liberalism and Social Action*, p. 17). Freedom, he believes, must include the means or power necessary to insure it in fact as well as in theory. It is possible, he asserts, to create a society where individuals participate equally in regulating common concerns. Such a society approaches the ideal of "community": It is united by the commitment of each member to the organized and intelligent management of the group's interests. Where individuals are united by the mood and style of action encouraged by pragmatism, social control is not experienced as external to the individual; it is part of his own activity.

Earlier I stated that Dewey's confidence in reason or education to reform social and economic institutions was not sufficiently justified even in terms of his own recognition of the connection between men's interests, beliefs, and their position in the economic structure of society. But there is a second sense in which we talk of the place of intelligence or reason in political life. Dewey has never imagined that reason is simply a technique for linking means to ends. Reason also must interpret the meaning of political phenomena. Given the number of different doctrines about, say, the meaning of the state, the temptation is strong, Dewey argues, "to drop all doctrines of this kind overboard, and stick to facts verifiably ascertained." But it is impossible to adopt such an attitude. "Political facts are not outside human desire and judgment. Change men's estimate of the *value* of existing political agencies and forms, and the latter change more or less. . . . Bodies of men are constantly engaged in attacking and trying to change some political habits, while other bodies of men are actively supporting and justifying them. It is mere pretense, then, to suppose that we can stick by the *de facto*, and not raise at some points the question of *de jure*: the question of by what right, the question of legitimacy" (*Public and Its Problems*, p. 6, Dewey's emphasis).

All political actors appeal ultimately to this or that doctrine, to some set of ideas. The success or failure of liberalism hinges on the clarity and validity of its main ideas. There can be no neat separation between ideas and action; however indirect and hidden, the former directs the latter. With this in mind, we should consider Dewey's theory of freedom. Not only is it central to his new liberalism, but it brings together the different parts of his political and social theory.

The problem of freedom is not one but a series of problems. We need to know how a man defines freedom, how he distinguishes the important from secondary or trivial freedoms, and how he relates freedom to other values. Dewey's theory of freedom is distinctive in that he combines a positive view of freedom as a form of self-perfection or growth with the negative conception of freedom as the absence of restraint. He uses both conceptions to answer questions about the different dimensions of freedom.[20]

20. For Dewey's general and distinct position among the many ideas of freedom, see Adler, *Idea of Freedom*, vols. 1, 2, particularly 1:594, for his classification of Dewey's theories. What I have in mind here is a distinction similar to Berlin's argument that the negative sense of freedom is involved in the effort to decide in which areas the individual should be allowed freedom of action to do whatever he wants, insofar as he does not interfere with others. The positive sense of freedom, Berlin argues, is an effort to answer the question of the nature of the control that makes a person be or do something different from what he otherwise might be or do. We can elaborate Berlin's distinction by suggesting that negative freedom is primarily an external freedom: It involves the relationships among men. Positive freedom appears more commonly as an

Negative freedom, he writes, "signifies freedom *from* subjection to the will and control of others; exemption from bondage; release from servitude; capacity to act without being exposed to direct obstructions or interference from others" (*Ethics of Democracy*, p. 437, Dewey's emphasis). But it must not be defined solely as the absence of restraint. Men must have the means, particularly economic means, to translate their desires into deeds. A second objection to the negative concept of freedom is more philosophical. Freedom is achieved only when a man's actions are intelligently informed; otherwise he may fail to achieve his purposes and will become the slave of his emotions and/or be manipulated by others.

Dewey views positive freedom as the better realization of one's self. This means individuality, growth in character, and the ability to control the environment and to solve problems, to work one's way out of difficulties. All these terms refer directly to Dewey's broad interpretation of education as the key to the good life. With such writers as Bertrand Russell, Robert Mac-Iver, and Isaiah Berlin, Dewey shares the belief that there are no final truths, and that freedom of action and opinion are essential in protecting the value of individual personality. But he differs in insisting that the quality of an individual's actions, not simply the absence of constraints, measures his freedom.

Dewey rejects the freedom-authority dichotomy of classical liberalism as an error analogous to the separation of the individual and the social. Freedom is to be found in a particular *type* of interaction between the individual and the group, between freedom and authority. "Liberty is that secure release and fulfillment of personal potentialities which take place only in rich and manifold association with others" (*Public and Its Problems*, p. 150).

Once it has been put into proper perspective, Dewey reasserts the merits of the negative concept of freedom. Since ideas and actions are interdependent, freedom as the positive growth of the individual requires also the power of free action. The absence of obstacles to men's actions is the means to realizing a higher freedom, the education of personality.

---

internal freedom: For Dewey, it means such things as ability, intelligence, or, in a word, character. Explaining this latter freedom is Dewey's main concern. See Berlin, *Four Essays on Liberty*, pp. 121-22.

Dewey's theory of freedom dovetails nicely with his theory of inquiry, with his ethical theory, and with his associations or interactions theory. Intelligent action, or instrumentalism, becomes the measure of freedom. Since the ethical goal is that activity which resolves a present problem while opening up the possibility for future growth, he maintains that the free man and the good man are the same.[21] Finally, freedom is identified with that type of association in which individuals use organized intelligence to improve social conditions.

In Dewey's words, freedom is of "varied plumage." Whenever we find almost all men approving some central political idea such as freedom, we can suspect that it means different things to different people. Even considering only the general categories of negative and positive freedom, it is evident that men want different and even contradictory things in the same name. It is not simply that freedom has become what one writer colorfully calls a "hurrah" word. Freedom is also used in a number of different contexts to discuss different types of problems.[22] In philosophy, for example, the problem of freedom often is discussed in terms of the controversy of free will or determinism. The classic instance is the theological precept that all men are free to act, but that at the same time God, since he is omniscient, knows how men will choose. But this problem does not occur simply in theology. Dewey poses an analogous issue in discussing the contrasting views of man's nature as either somehow "original" or as determined by the environment. In political discourse, it is common to focus on the relational or juristic sense of freedom: One man's freedom is measured by the restrictions imposed on him by others.

One of the merits of Dewey's social and political philosophy is that he sees the problem of freedom as multidimensional. He has attempted to develop a systematic theory of freedom which takes account of the many sides of freedom. In a 1928 essay, "Philosophies of Freedom," he examines three philosophies of freedom dominant in the modern world: freedom as choice, freedom as power, and freedom as reason. Evaluating the insights of each, he presents a reconstructed version of freedom

21. Dewey, *Outlines of Ethics*, p. 164.
22. Dewey, *On Experience, Nature, and Freedom*, p. 262; Spitz, *Essays in the Liberal Idea of Freedom*, pp. 115-16; compare Cranston, *Freedom*, pp. 81-82.

in which all three elements play an equally important role. Since he in effect combines the elements of choice and reason in the notion of freedom as rational conduct, his doctrine of freedom can be examined conveniently under this heading and under the heading freedom as power.

Dewey's interest in the problem of free will is evident within the larger context of his organic view of society. Every individual, he argues, is born into a pre-existing system of "deeply grooved interactions" that make up society. In this interaction Dewey is quite clear that the environment plays the stronger role. *Human Nature and Conduct* argues that the formation of a person's desires and aims cannot be understood apart from a sociopsychological study of human nature, i.e., the habits and beliefs which he acquires from his environment. Against this background, Dewey considers the dispute of free will or determinism. His analysis is structured around the meaning of choice. Any system of praise and blame, reward and punishment, presumes that men author their own actions. The idea of freedom and the very possibility of moral responsibility are linked closely. There is "an inexpugnable feeling that choice *is* freedom." But closer examination reveals choice to be part of a man's "concrete make-up of habits, desires, and purposes." At this point, the determinist asserts that a man's actions are decided by his acquired nature as a product of the environment. If this is true, Dewey asserts that choice, an important element of freedom, would be meaningless; man would be a "puppet" without any acts he could call his own (*On Experience, Nature, and Freedom*, pp. 262, 264).

At first glance, Dewey's own account of human nature seems to resemble the determinist position. Indeed, he agrees with the determinist objection against some sort of original nature which accounts solely for man's actions. But Dewey argues that choice is continuous with, not reducible to, a man's habits or modes of behavior as products of his interaction with the environment. A man's history is not all of one piece; every man has a "variable life history" and "undergoes varied and opposed experiences." Choice becomes important for deciding among preferences by "the forecast of the consequences of acting upon the various competing preferences." This is possible because man has the power of deliberation; choice, however influenced, is not determined.[23] Dewey's theory of human nature leads to the conclusion that an intelligent self, in control of the environment, is an important part of freedom. "To foresee future objective alternatives and to be able by deliberation to choose one of them and thereby weigh its chances in the struggle for future existence, measures our freedom. It is assumed sometimes that if it can be shown that deliberation is determined by character and conditions, there is no freedom. This is like saying that because a flower comes from root and stem it cannot bear fruit. The question is not what are the antecedents of deliberation and choice, but what are their consequences? What do they do that is distinctive? The answer is that they give us all the control of future possibilities which is open to us. And this control is the crux of our freedom. Without it, we are pushed from behind. With it, we walk in the light" (*Human Nature and Conduct*, p. 285).

The foregoing clearly anticipates Dewey's belief that freedom is advanced not merely by any choice, but by those choices which are informed intelligently. A man may be free to choose and free to act, but this is no guarantee his freedom is genuine. Those who fail to understand freedom as reason fail to recognize that men's choices and actions may be foolish, blind, and impulsive ("Philosophies of Freedom," p. 273). "*Actual* freedom lies in the realization of that end which actually satisfies. An end may be freely adopted, and yet its actual working out may result not in freedom, but in slavery. It may result in rendering the agent more subject to his passions, less able to direct his own conduct, and more cramped and feeble in powers. Only that end which executed really effects greater energy and comprehensiveness of character makes for actual freedom. In a word, only the good man, the man who is truly realizing his individuality, is free, in the positive sense of that word" (*Outlines of Ethics*, p. 164, Dewey's emphasis).

Certain dangers attend the definition of freedom as rational conduct. A man may be required to act in a manner defined as "rational" by someone else or by the majority. Forced to behave rationally, the individual is told that he is "really free." However, Dewey's doctrine of freedom as rational conduct must be

23. Dewey, "Philosophies of Freedom," in *On Experience, Nature, and Freedom*, pp. 262–67.

distinguished from the doctrine of "enforceable rational freedom." Maurice Cranston captures the major difference between the two: "*Rational freedom* finds freedom in self-discipline. *Enforceable rational freedom* finds freedom in discipline" (Cranston's emphasis).[24] For Dewey, there is a necessary link between freedom as growth in developing preferences into intelligent choices and the individual's freedom to choose and to act for himself. Growth in individuality and rational conduct is not something that can be done *for* the individual, it is something that must happen *to* him through his own participation. Since reason is instrumental to reorganizing new experiences and problems, choice is not something fixed. Freedom is "a growth, an attainment." The individual's political education and freedom require that he himself learn by choosing, responding to, and utilizing the conditions present in the environment. "No individual can make the determination for anyone else; nor can he make it for himself all at once and forever." A man's freedom is one with his individuality. Freedom to choose his own direction enlarges the individual's range of action. Since the processes of action and choice are both educational, this in turn makes choice more intelligent. But individual growth does not occur in a vacuum; there must be favorable social, political, and economic conditions. Only from the standpoint of the relationship between rational choice *and* action can the importance of political and economic freedom not be "an addendum or afterthought."[25]

Dewey's discussion of freedom and politics is still mainly philosophical. His definition of freedom as rational conduct has both a negative and a positive side. Negatively, it leads him to criticize classical liberalism's definition of freedom and how to attain it. The old liberalism views freedom simply as the power to act once the obstacles of "oppressive measures, tyrannical

24. Cranston, *Freedom*, p. 21. In *Problems of Men*, Dewey writes, "The idea of forcing men to be free is an old idea, but by nature it is opposed to freedom. Freedom is not something that can be handed to men as a gift from outside, whether by old-fashioned dynastic benevolent despotisms or by new-fashioned dictatorships, whether of the proletarian or of the fascist order. It is something which can be had only as individuals participate in winning it, and this fact, rather than some particular political mechanism, is the essence of democratic liberalism" (p. 132).

25. Dewey, "Philosophies of Freedom," p. 275; *Individualism*, pp. 166–67; *On Experience, Nature, and Freedom*, p. 269.

laws, and modes of government" are removed. Such a view of freedom is incorrect in meaning and in techniques proposed for guaranteeing it. First, the theory thinks of "individuals as endowed with an equipment of fixed and ready-made capacities." This idea neglects the importance of the surrounding social medium in influencing desires and impulses. Second, although the liberal school commonly is criticized for being too individualistic, "it would be equally pertinent to say that it was not 'individualistic' enough." In other words, the philosophy of liberalism removed many obstructions to, and arbitrary restraints upon, men's actions, but this does not automatically promote the "general liberation of all individuals" (*On Experience, Nature, and Freedom*, pp. 269, 271). One need only consider the consequences of the economic doctrine of laissez-faire to appreciate this point.

Dewey's analysis of the significance of choice as an element of freedom leads to the conclusion that intelligence is as basic as restricting arbitrary power. In "Democracy and Educational Administration," he states: "Democracy is so often and so naturally associated in our minds with freedom of *action*, forgetting the importance of freed intelligence which is necessary to direct and to warrant freedom of action. Unless freedom of individual action has intelligence and informed conviction back of it, its manifestation is almost sure to result in confusion and disorder. The democratic idea of freedom is not the right of each individual to *do* as he pleases, even if it be qualified by adding 'provided he does not interfere with the same freedom on the part of others.' While the idea is not always, not often enough, expressed in words, the basic freedom is that of freedom of *mind* and whatever degree of freedom of action and experience is necessary to produce freedom of intelligence" (*Problems of Men*, p. 61, Dewey's emphasis). Central to this vision is the demand for a form of *praxis* that brings out the qualities characteristic of an individual growing in self-direction and self-fulfillment. "We are free not because of what we statically are, but in as far as we are becoming different from what we have been" (*On Experience, Nature, and Freedom*, p. 280).

Since a person can grow only through his experiences, a man must be free to act. But Dewey finds a shallowness in that phrase. "To say that a man is free to choose to walk while the only walk he can take will lead him over a precipice is to strain words as well as facts" (*Human Nature and Conduct*, p. 279). Wealth, education, and privilege all operate to deny freedom to the less fortunate where the latter have no means to protect themselves or to better their position. Therefore, liberty must be understood as "power, effective power to do specific things. There is no such thing as liberty in general; liberty, so to speak, at large. If one wants to know what the condition of liberty is at a given time, one has to examine what persons *can* do and what they *cannot* do. The moment one examines the question from the standpoint of effective action, it becomes evident that the demand for liberty is a demand for power, either for possession of powers of action not already possessed or for retention and expansion of powers already possessed."[26]

Thus, freedom is one with the *means* necessary for a man to accomplish his ends. The new liberalism, or the new freedom, promises individuals an *equal* chance to realize their purposes or desires.[27] Dewey's definition of freedom as power justifies a reform politics geared to guaranteeing equality of opportunity and, although he never spells it out, to guaranteeing equality of power to the extent necessary to insure all men freedom of action.

At least since de Tocqueville argued that men's taste for equality may become so strong that individuality and freedom will be lost, various writers have maintained that liberty and

26. Dewey, "Liberty and Social Control," in *Problems of Men*, p. 111 (Dewey's emphasis). Hayek strongly criticizes Dewey's identification of freedom with the means necessary to achieve one's purposes. He argues that it is "only another name for the old demand for the equal distribution of wealth." He believes this demand deprives men of freedom by leading to social engineering and to increased centralization of political power. However, Hayek really does not answer Dewey's objection that one cannot merely trust to the operation of the free market for establishment of a distribution of liberties that benefits most men (*Road to Serfdom*, p. 26). A different argument for keeping clear the distinction between freedom and means is offered by Fosdick. She argues that the state can play a major role in establishing a more desirable system of liberties and restraints. Redistribution of means, she argues, is one way this can be accomplished. However, she, too, believes that liberty must be kept distinct from means; otherwise, we lose sight of the fact that even though men may enjoy economic equality, they may not be free in the negative sense of the absence of controls or restraints on their actions (*What Is Liberty?*, pp. 120, 79).

27. Dewey, "Liberty and Social Control," in *Problems of Men*, p. 116.

equality are incompatible goals. An increase in one, they argue, must be traded for a decrease in the other. More exactly, a policy such as socialism can produce greater economic equality among *all* men and increase the freedom of some and perhaps *most* men. But socialism also requires restraints or controls which limit the freedom of *other* men.[28]

Dewey responds to the problem of the relationship between liberty and equality in two ways. First, he argues that the choice is not between liberty and equality; it is a choice between certain liberties and certain equalities along with the concomitant restraints. Second, he urges a more generous and constructive view of liberty and equality as complementary ideals in defining a particular type of community.

Dewey's first response builds on his view of freedom as power. Since liberty is relative to the distribution of power in society, the liberty enjoyed by some is accompanied by restraints elsewhere. *"The system of liberties that exists at any time is always the system of restraints or controls that exists at that time.* No one can do anything except in relation to what others can do and cannot do"(*Problems of Men*, p. 113, Dewey's emphasis). The choice between capitalism and socialism, for example, is posed falsely if this means choosing between "collectivism" and "individualism" or between liberty and equality. The issue is not control of the economy; rather, it is which system of control and accompanying liberties is desired. Capitalism is a system of private control and economic inequalities which purchases the economic liberty of the few at the expense of the many. Therefore, liberty for most men is not the antithesis of economic equality; the former depends on the latter.

Dewey argues also that the inequalities existing in society should reflect the real differences among men, not the artificial inequalities imposed by birth and by institutions that automatically benefit some at the expense of others. Even the natural inequalities should be modified by laws and by institutions in order that the less fortunate do not suffer serious handicaps and hardships. This adds to the discussion of liberty and equality the third value of the democratic triad—fraternity. Those who set up an opposition between liberty and equality have a

28. Fosdick, *What Is Liberty?*, p. 12.

narrow understanding of freedom *in* the community. Equality does not mean simply equality of opportunity; it means "the unhampered share which each individual member of the community has in the consequences of associated action." In this sense, liberty and equality are complementary: Everyone should enjoy the liberty of being an "individualized self making a distinctive contribution and enjoying in its own way the fruits of association" (*Public and Its Problems*, p. 150). Fraternity or community is the ideal which unites liberty and equality. This vision of the good life, where relationships are marked by harmony and respect for the uniqueness of each person, underlies Dewey's idea of freedom. The fullness of the democratic creed can be realized only within a community bound together by a common good as each individual helps direct the affairs of the whole.

Positive freedom is essential. It gives men the method for readjusting external relationships to promote the freedom of each person. Positive and political freedoms are united. Only through democracy, with its emphasis on participation, inquiry, and communication, can men become part of a community intelligently regulating its affairs. *Political education is both the means and the substance of freedom.*

Dewey's abiding faith in the dignity and ability of each personality makes him optimistic about the development of a community of free men. Dissatisfied with formal definitions of freedom, he attempts to shore up liberty by making power, reason, and certain equalities integral parts of life. But even those who agree with him must note the confusion and mistakes in his arguments. It can be argued, for instance, that Dewey uses too loosely the word "freedom." In making it stand for "reason," for a man's "better self," and for moral "growth," he increases the ambiguity of a word already difficult to define, even if we grant that his multifaceted view of freedom is an effort to deal with problems in a variety of contexts. Other flaws in his idea of freedom are more important. In effect, he shifts many critical problems from the issue of an individual's relationship within the community to the technological issue of how society successfully solves its problems. As a result, certain key issues about freedom such as the consequences of coercion are ignored or misconstrued. An instrumentalist examines freedom in terms of consequences. Freedom is not simply the absence of restraints or the existence of alternative opportunities; it is the realization of choice in action. Positive freedom means successful problem solving. But the effect of this teaching is to divert attention away from how regulations and controls impinge on and restrict the individual's freedom of action.

The argument begins on a persuasive note. To decry all authority and social control is to stifle social and economic reforms necessary for most men to be free in fact. And I have no quarrel with Dewey's contention that laws and social controls upon some men can liberate other men. But Dewey is saying something more than this. It is a mistake, he argues, to view freedom and control as distinct experiences; they are complementary parts of the effort to solve problems through collective action. In "Authority and Resistance to Social Change," he states that the question is the "*relation* between authority and liberty." To view them as antithetical postpones the search for ways to unite individual and collective action. Since the individual's fate is bound to his environment and to favorable social conditions, Dewey is offering a new way of looking at freedom and authority. "In effect, authority stands for stability of social organization by means of which direction and support are given to individuals; while individual freedom stands for the forces by which change is intentionally brought about."[29] Dewey has shifted the problem of freedom to the issue of how to direct social change. Scientific method, then, becomes the answer to the issue of freedom's relation to authority.

Dewey relies on the model of authority in science to support his contention that there is an "organic union" between freedom and authority. The authority of science is not arbitrary; it "issues from and is based upon collective activity, cooperatively organized" (*Problems of Men*, p. 101). Science is an activity requiring that men share their ideas and submit their findings to the community of scientists for verification. Without cooperation and collective efforts, science would not be possible. Therefore, membership in the scientific community and submission to its authority does not restrict the individual

29. Dewey, "Authority and Resistance to Social Change," in *Problems of Men*, p. 94; see also p. 101.

scientist. Authority is not experienced as external to his own purposes; it is part of the scientist's own activity and gives it meaning. In short, the authority of the principles and beliefs found in the scientific community stems from cooperative inquiries; the authority itself is a cooperative authority. This has implications for other areas. "The thesis that the operation of cooperative intelligence as displayed in science is a working model of the union of freedom and authority does not slight the fact that the method has operated up to the present in a limited and relatively technical area. On the contrary, it emphasizes that fact. If the method of intelligence had been employed in any large field in the comprehensive and basic area of the relations of human beings to one another in social life and institutions, there would be no present need for our argument. The contrast between the restricted scope of its use and the possible range of its application to human relations—political, economic, and moral—is outstanding enough to be depressing. It is this very contrast that serves to define the great problem that lies before us" (*Problems of Men*, pp. 107-8).

Dewey's arguments here are the same as his analysis of authority in the classroom. When social control or authority is rooted in cooperative inquiries, it is equivalent to the "moving spirit of the whole group." The control is social; therefore, it does not restrict individual freedom. The ideal community would regulate its affairs through widespread participation, operating the same as the individual who intelligently directs his own affairs. The goal is an educational one: the extension of the area of reasonableness.

The persuasiveness of Dewey's thesis derives largely from his argument that what is true for science can be true for politics. But alternative viewpoints suggest that the scientific community is more complicated than Dewey imagines. For example, Thomas Kuhn's *The Structure of Scientific Revolutions* presents a conception of science and scientists which challenges Dewey's model of authority. Kuhn points out that every scientific field possesses a "paradigm" or model based on its widely recognized achievements. This paradigm tells the scientist which entities exist in the world, how explanations and laws must be shaped, and how research problems are likely to look. According to Kuhn, a person entering the scientific profession spends much of his time learning the postulates and rules of the reigning paradigm. And most normal scientific activity involves solving puzzles within the framework of this general model—gathering new facts, fitting them into the paradigm, and articulating the paradigm theory.

Two points are especially significant in Kuhn's account of science. First, he points out that the normal activity of puzzle solving rarely involves the testing of long-accepted beliefs. "The scientific enterprise as a whole does from time to time prove useful, open up new territory, display order, and test long-accepted beliefs. Nevertheless, the *individual* engaged on a normal research problem *is almost never doing any one of these things.* Once engaged, his motivation is of a rather different sort. What then challenges him is the conviction that, if only he is skillful enough, he will succeed in solving a puzzle that no one before has solved or solved so well" (p. 38, Kuhn's emphasis).

This picture is quite different from Dewey's account of science as a venture in which men determine equally and cooperatively which beliefs and rules are to control their activities. In Kuhn's account, the individual learns the rules; he does not make them. Kuhn argues also that the scientific community uses its authority to require acceptance of the major paradigm by its members, especially its newer ones. "Normal science, the activity in which most scientists inevitably spend almost all their time, is predicated on the assumption that the scientific community knows what the world is like. Much of the success of the enterprise derives from the community's willingness to defend that assumption, if necessary at considerable cost. Normal science, for example, often suppresses fundamental novelties because they are necessarily subversive of its basic commitments" (p. 5). The scientific community is open sufficiently so that it can switch from an old to a new paradigm whenever necessary to solve new and critical problems within a particular scientific field. But it is not necessary here to describe Kuhn's account of how such scientific revolutions or paradigm switches occur.[30] What is clear is that Kuhn views the authority

30. For an analysis of how this part of Kuhn's account of science might be significant for understanding the enterprise of political science, see Sheldon Wolin, "Paradigms and Political Theories," in King and Parekh, eds., *Politics and Experience*, pp. 125-52.

exercised by the scientific community as much more rigid than does Dewey.

Judging the adequacy of Dewey's or Kuhn's conception of science can be best left to the philosophers of science. I will not try to referee that contest. But two things are evident. Should Kuhn's arguments be correct, Dewey's strong reliance on science as an example to support his case for a cooperative authority which liberates the individual, even though it governs much of his behavior, may be a weak analogy indeed for discussing political authority. More important, whatever is true of authority in the scientific community cannot really settle the question of how we are to understand and judge the exercise of political power. Dewey's preoccupation with scientific method is a central weakness in his entire political theory. It blurs the distinctly political context within which the problem of freedom and authority arises whenever we are concerned with citizens, not scientists.

The scientific world and the political world are different; political problems are not like problems in nature. So far as the scientist is concerned, the question of how to build a pollution-free engine, for instance, involves mainly the possession of sufficient knowledge to guide a series of instrumental actions. For the scientist, power is simply an instrument or technique for controlling the interaction of natural forces to produce a desired outcome. In marked contrast, political problems involve antagonisms among men who may want to go in different directions, or who agree on a general end but disagree about the means. Any political action which relies on power to resolve a conflict or "problem" must also impose the answer on some men. When man uses power to solve problems in nature, he simply enforces his will on it. But the exercise of political power means that some men impose their will on that of other men.

The chief advantage of the negative idea of freedom is that it calls attention to the coercive element in any organized system of control. Freedom is a relational problem; it involves conflicts among men, and one man's freedom can be measured by the power other men have over him.[31] Negative freedom focuses attention on the need to justify social controls in terms of the

31. Cranston, in fairness, reminds us that "the word 'liberty' has its least ambiguity in political use in times of centralized oppression" (Freedom, p. 8).

liberty lost, or, more accurately, the liberties lost by some men and the goods gained by others. In each case, some price must be paid. The price may be worth paying, of course. But we need the ideas of authority and freedom as distinct types of experiences in order to confront such issues. Dewey's notion of a cooperative authority which views control and freedom as complementary makes it difficult to meet such questions head-on.

Despite Dewey's arguments, a tension remains between liberty and equality. For example, the state may provide each person with an equal opportunity for good health care, but its program of compulsory health insurance not only regulates doctors' fees but requires that workers contribute to it. This regulates, or interferes with, the freedom of doctors to charge as much as the market will bear and the freedom of the worker to spend his income as he wishes. Freedom is not the only value, of course, and for many people the values of socialized medicine may have more merit than the liberty sacrificed. But Dewey's theory of socially organized intelligent control leads to the position that no freedom has been sacrificed. Dewey wants to shift the emphasis from the absence of restraints to a notion of positive freedom. This is a mistake. Freedom *from*, not freedom *to*, is the primary criterion of liberty. Economic equality may solve the problem of means; education and the spread of intelligence may solve the need for intelligently guided action; but neither of these conditions necessarily solves the problem of freedom. Giovanni Sartori rightly insists that "Equality is a form of freedom only in the sense that it is a 'condition of freedom.' And to say that one thing is a condition of another is not to say that they are the same thing . . . an illiterate is probably in no condition to act like a free man, but it cannot be inferred from this that once he has learned to read and write he has become free. It depends. Similarly, granted that equality is a condition of freedom, it does not follow from this that by having been made equal we become *ipso facto* and for this very reason free. It depends: and above all it depends on what type of master has seen to making us equal."[32] As long as conflicts occur between the individual and the whole, controls must be viewed

32. Sartori, *Democratic Theory*, p. 348.

as impositions, and authority must be recognized as a restriction.[33]

Dewey's revision of the liberal idea of freedom exhibits strengths and flaws characteristic of his pragmatist political philosophy. The merits of his position are traceable mainly to the pragmatist's insistence that performance counts. This is evident in what may be Dewey's simplest point; namely, a theory of liberty defined as the absence of restraint risks setting up a false opposition between freedom and law, liberty and government. If unrestrained, some men will be ready always to invade the freedoms of others. Where laws decrease the amount and frequency of such invasions, the net amount of freedom is increased. It is a modest point, but Dewey is right to insist on it

33. In a 1919 essay "Force and Coercion," Dewey attempts to develop a theory of power in strict accordance with the logic of instrumentalism. Therefore, he argues that the only basis for distinguishing among the various forms of power is their relative "efficiency." Power, he argues, is simply a neutral term referring to "effective means of operation." When power is wasteful—that is, when it fails to achieve purposes—it is "violence." And coercion and law are said to occupy a middle ground. "Coercive force occupies, we may fairly say, a middle place between power as energy and power as violence. To turn to the right as an incident of locomotion is a case of power: of means deplored in behalf of an end. To run amuck in the street is a case of violence. To use energy to make a man observe the rule of the road is a case of coercive force. . . . Constraint or coercion, in other words, is an incident of a situation under certain conditions—namely, where the means for the realization of an end are not naturally at hand, so that energy has to be spent in order to make some power into a means for the realization of an end." The effect of this doctrine is simply to turn the problem of political power into a case of efficiency. "The only question which can be raised about the justification of force is that of comparative efficiency and economy in its use." Liberty itself is to be assessed merely as an "efficiency factor." *Characters and Events*, 2:782-89.

In this essay and throughout the World War I period, Dewey's instrumentalism blinded him to the fact that political power is not simply in the hands of efficiency experts or impartial social engineers. Bourne, a sharp critic of Dewey's support of the war, understands clearly the limitations of this side of Dewey's doctrine. "Dewey's philosophy is inspiring enough for a society at peace, prosperous and with a fund of progressive good-will." But Bourne adds immediately that "this careful adaptation of means to desired ends, this experimental working out of control over brute forces and dead matter in the interests of communal life depends on a store of rationality, and is effective only where there is strong desire for progress." Bourne's own suspicion was that it was only the school, the institution to which Dewey first applied his philosophy, that ever came close to meeting these requirements. *War and Intellectuals*, pp. 55-56.

A modest but nevertheless unsuccessful attempt to defend Dewey's instrumentalist conception of force is Hu Shih, "Political Philosophy of Instrumentalism," in *Philosopher of the Common Man*, ed. Sidney Ratner, pp. 205-19.

as a warning against those who use the formula of negative liberty to negate liberty, i.e., by protesting against all laws.

Pragmatism's conception of the individual as an actor and as a social being also enables Dewey to tie more closely to the condition of freedom the reasons men value freedom. That is, the condition of freedom is one of non-interference with the individual; the value of such a condition is the type of life it enables him to live. The absence of restraint is important for a sense of self-mastery. A man must feel that his purposes and not someone else's govern his life. Dewey's complaint against negative freedom is that it does not capture fully why men value freedom. In this connection, Dewey is largely successful. He reminds us again of the value of man's communal life. Following such writers as Rousseau and T. H. Green, Dewey argues persuasively that a person is not a self-enclosed entity. A man's personality and behavior, his beliefs and loyalties, his successes and failures, and his opportunities are all influenced by his interactions with others. Dewey then goes beyond traditional liberal arguments to maintain that "being an individual" is itself problematic. To realize oneself, to be free, depends on the nature of a man's interactions. The condition of freedom, that is, security against coercion, may only require the forbearance of others, but the use of that freedom requires their support. The main attraction of positive liberty is that it describes a man who is acting as a fully *human* being, rather than just a man who is simply left alone.

Dewey's contributions to the discussion of freedom are substantial, but he obscures some crucial issues. Critics of positive liberty are correct in arguing that positive liberty, more easily than negative liberty, risks turning into the opposite of freedom. This has occurred in the literature of freedom in two common ways. First, the language of self-mastery or self-realization has imagined the individual divided into two selves. This has been used to defend the coercion of the emotional or ignorant self to free the better self, i.e., men will be "forced to be free." Up to this point, Dewey warns against drawing such a conclusion from the idea of positive liberty. Self-discipline, he insists, is not to be confused with enforced self-discipline.

Positive liberty can lead to its opposite in another way. Here Dewey is not attentive enough to the implications of his position. Coercive positive liberty usually is tied to the assumptions that the ends of all rational persons are essentially harmonious, that conflicts are due mainly to the clash between the rational and the irrational, and that in principle such clashes can be avoided.[34] Although Dewey does not make these specific assumptions, his somewhat breathtaking thesis that authority and freedom are reconciled in the experiential activity of "intelligent problem solving" resembles them enough to justify alarm. Clearly, Dewey does not draw the conclusions of advocates of coercive freedom. But he is not sensitive to the dangers attending his belief that a greater reliance on intelligence will lead to a society with substantial harmony.

34. Compare Berlin, *Four Essays on Liberty*, pp. 134, 154. For an appreciative but critical discussion of Berlin's theory, see Macpherson, *Democratic Theory*, pp. 95–119.

6. Democracy and the
Participatory Society

RECENTLY, political theorists are paying closer attention to the distinction between the exercise and the control of political power. Understood primarily as a theory of representative government, democracy requires a set of constitutional and political arrangements whereby the people can check or limit the state's power. In this view, the people do not govern but rather choose their governors. The main concern is with the accountability of the few to the many, rather than with extending the activity of ruling to as many people as possible. In contrast, theories of participatory democracy argue that the popular exercise of power, not only in elections but in day-to-day decision making, is critical to the development and growth of the individual as both man and citizen. The distinction, as drawn by one recent author, is between the "politics of power" and the "politics of participation." The former gives to a few men the primary responsibility for making authoritative decisions in society. These few may be elected; nevertheless, they are the active citizens, the leaders. Popular political participation in elections, for example, is considered significant not as a record of the *vox populi* with all this implies about direction as well as control from below, but as a method for legitimating the

100

power of those few who do direct society.(In contrast, participation means "group undertakings which not only involve a common membership but rely on this membership to initiate and direct those undertakings.")

The most famous critic of participatory democracy and classical theory is Joseph Schumpeter. His more realistic definition of democracy describes it as "that institutional arrangement for arriving at political decisions in which individuals acquire the power to decide by means of a competitive struggle for the people's vote." What Schumpeter and others argue is that the ideal of participatory democracy is unrealistic and, perhaps, even undesirable. The majority of citizens, it is contended, are apathetic, disinterested, and uninformed about politics. The ideal of the enlightened and concerned democratic citizen directing public affairs is denounced as a myth. A realistic democratic theory must begin with citizens as they are, not with citizens as we might wish they were. Unrealistic expectations for democracy only encourage cynicism and disappointment. Moreover, attempts to mobilize masses of apathetic citizens, only marginally committed to the principles of democracy, could disrupt the political order. The "irony of democracy," according to two writers, is that democracy's success depends on the active few, the elite who do play according to the rules of the democratic game.[1]

No one familiar with studies of public opinion or voting behavior can casually dismiss the arguments of those who insist on a more realistic view of democracy. But there are problems. Critics charge the realists with a misplaced trust in the elite's willingness to abide by democratic rules when their power is seriously threatened or their decisions widely disapproved, as in the case of the Vietnam war. Also, there is no warrant, it is held, for assuming that because a political system is stable it is adequately meeting the needs of its citizens.[2]

1. Pranger, *Eclipse of Citizenship*, pp. 3, 12; Schumpeter, *Capitalism, Socialism, and Democracy*, p. 269; Dye and Zeigler, *The Irony of Democracy*, p. 2.
2. There is an important discussion of voting behavior and democratic theory in Berleson, *Voting*, esp. pp. 305-23. For criticisms of the revisionist theorists of democracy, see Bachrach, *The Theory of Democratic Elitism*, Pateman, *Participation and Democratic Theory*, Kaufman, *The Radical Liberal*, pp. 60-67, and Flacks, "On Uses of Participatory Democracy," pp. 701-8.

These and other objections to the realists can be best discussed here by considering Dewey's criticisms of Walter Lippmann, one of the first theorists to demand a more realistic theory of democracy. But it also needs to be noted that we may not be faced with an either/or choice. That is, it is conceivable that the arrangements and values described by participatory democracy complement the values of representative democracy. One theory may not preclude certain key points in the other. In the case of John Stuart Mill, for example, the value of the individual's participation in decision making was combined with a defense of the value of constitutional arrangements for limiting the power of representatives.

Mill set forth two major defenses of democracy. First, he viewed democracy as a form of government for controlling the uses—and, more important, for limiting the possible abuses—of political power. From this perspective, democratic procedures and freedoms are important mainly as a means of self-protection. "Men, as well as women, do not need political rights in order that they may govern, but in order that they may not be misgoverned."[3] This protective principle is characteristic of liberalism. The limited or, more exactly, the constitutional state is less likely to use power arbitrarily or capriciously. Requiring the state to exercise its power through due process partly balances the distribution of power between citizen and government. Indeed, the motto of liberalism or representative democracy might well be "All power to no one." Rather, proceduralism and constitutionalism become the final seats of authority.

Mill's first defense of democracy has been the one most commonly adopted by later democratic theorists. It is felt to fit best what we now know about the obstacles to mass participation and the large role played by elites in corporate society. By controlling the way power is acquired—through a competitive struggle for the people's vote—it is hoped that one can control the way it is exercised. But Mill himself argued that there was a "superior" defense of democracy. The real test of a good government is its contribution to the citizen's political education. "The first element of good government, therefore, being the virtue and intelligence of the human beings com-

3. Mill, *Utilitarianism, Liberty, and Representative Government*, p. 391.

posing the community, the most important point of excellence which any form of government can possess is to promote the virtue and intelligence of the people themselves. . . . The government which does this the best has every likelihood of being the best in all other respects, since it is on these qualities, so far as they exist in the people, that all possibility of goodness in the practical operations of the government depends" (p. 259). Democracy is now defended as a way of developing the intellectual and the moral capacities of an individual. By making a man responsible for some of the business of governing, democracy increases his competence and his feeling for the public or social interest. Political participation forces the individual to consider interests other than his own and to frame his personal preferences in terms of larger principles. Politics is now seen as more than a piece of machinery for advancing or protecting one's private interests. Rather, participation is felt to be critical to the development of civic virtue, whereby power is shared widely and individuals are socially minded.[4] Mill's writings discuss a number of ways in which participation might become more widespread in society. His early writings emphasize political participation at the local level. His assumption is that individuals are more interested and better equipped to play a role in local politics. His later writings suggest that participation can be increased by extending the ideal to cover other areas of society, especially industry. The "improving" effect of participation in local government and the work place would, Mill believed, increase the citizen's competence to judge the performance of his representatives.

Since pragmatism is a philosophy of experience, it is not surprising that Dewey, like Mill, makes public participation and political education key features of the democratic society. In pursuing this theme, Dewey also engages in a polemic against those writers who define democracy solely as a form of government.[5] Rather, democracy is a participatory society.

4. Ibid., pp. 272-74; for a discussion of this aspect of Mill's political writings, see H. J. McClosky, "Mill's Liberalism," in *Essays in the History of Political Thought*, ed. Kramnick, pp. 371-84.

5. To the liberal concern with constitutional controls and the democratic emphasis on popular participation, Dewey adds a third dimension—the rationality or reasonableness of the political process in terms of its probable decisions. For a discussion of various democratic theories in terms of these

Participation, he stresses, cannot be limited to one set of experiences; it must include other authority structures within ✳ society. Democracy is nothing less than a way of life, inseparable from the customs, occupations, education—the entire culture—of a society. Dewey's strategy for realizing participatory democracy is to link the meaning of democracy to this idea of a participatory society; participation in other areas of society in addition to the political can add to the individual's understanding of the relationship between public affairs and his private life. More important, the participatory society transforms the context within which the representative political system works, better preparing the individual to judge the performance of representatives and to participate himself when opportunities become available. Political education is not one but many processes.

THE DEMOCRATIC PUBLIC

In 1927, Dewey published *The Public and Its Problems*, a work which defines democracy in terms of the citizen's participation in the direct formation of the public interest. Dewey's book had been preceded by Walter Lippmann's two studies of the public's role in a democracy, *Public Opinion* and *The Phantom Public*. Comparisons between Lippmann's and Dewey's works are almost inevitable, since they deal with a similar issue but arrive at widely different conclusions. Also, Lippmann had been influenced strongly by pragmatist philosophy, especially by William James,[6] while Dewey acknowledged a debt to Lippmann in his own study of the public.

Lippmann borrows from pragmatism the preoccupation with intelligence as a guide to action. In arguing that the public is incapable of meeting the demands of informed action, he begins *Public Opinion* by contrasting the "picture in our heads" with the situation in the objective or real world. Censorship, reliance on stereotypes, limited time and interest—all intervene between the events in the real world and men's opinions about these

three dimensions, see Kettler, "Politics of Social Change," in *Bias of Pluralism*, ed. Connolly, pp. 213–49.

6. Forcey discusses Lippmann's pragmatism and his relationship to James in *Crossroads of Liberalism*, pp. 96–97.

events. This produces a partial and distorted image of reality. Although he does without the metaphysics, Lippmann in effect argues the traditional Platonic distinction between knowledge and opinion. Most men, he believes, see merely shadows on the walls of the cave—an inferior and imperfect image of events in the real world of politics. Therefore, when the government relies too heavily on public opinion to guide its actions, it inevitably makes mistakes (pp. 18-19).

Lippmann does not condemn the public for its ignorance; rather, he attacks those theorists who expect the public to have a "knowledge beyond their reach." He traces this demand to the "original democrats" and the old democratic philosophy. This philosophy, says Lippmann, assumed that political power derived from the right origin—the public—would insure good government. The democrat upheld the dignity of man, but he "risked the dignity of man on one very precarious assumption, that he would exhibit that dignity instinctively in wise laws and good government" (p. 197). But the public does not always choose wisely. When leaders are overly sensitive to the mood of the public, Lippmann contends, democratic government becomes feeble and incompetent.

Lippmann proposes that the old democratic philosophy be replaced by a new theory which recognizes that the public can judge the soundness of a decision only "after the event." In other words, political participation, or popular rule (as distinct from popular control), is harmful and needs to be dropped from what Lippmann was later to call the public philosophy. As "outsiders," the public's role is to say yes or no to the performance of the "insiders," to those who daily administer social affairs. Democracy needs the organization of expert "intelligence bureaus" to advise the government and "to make the invisible world visible to the citizens of a modern state" (p. 202).

In Lippmann's new democracy, government is to be judged by its performance or consequences. Men desire democratic government not for its own sake, he contends, but for its results.

> The democratic fallacy has been its preoccupation with
> the origin of government rather than with the
> processes and results. . . . But no amount of regulation
> at the source of a river will completely control its

behavior, and while democrats have been absorbed in trying to find a good mechanism for originating social power, that is to say a good mechanism of voting and representation, they neglected almost every other interest of men. For no matter how power originates, the crucial interest is in how power is exercised. What determines the quality of civilization is the use made of power. And that use cannot be controlled at the source.

The criteria which you then apply to government are whether it is producing a certain minimum of health, of decent housing, of material necessities, of education, of freedom, of pleasures, of beauty, not simply whether at the sacrifice of all these things, it vibrates to the self-centered opinions that happen to be floating around in men's minds (pp. 196–97).

Lippmann's theory is best described as democratic elitism, a term developed by Peter Bachrach. Democratic elitism represents a "revolt from the masses." Where earlier versions of democracy insisted on the equality of men, at least in the sense that every individual was to be encouraged to take part in making decisions, democratic elitism insists on the inequality of individual competence and restricts decision making to an elite. The masses, not elites, are now suspect when it comes to having and using power—thus, Lippmann's proposal to rely on "expert leadership." Lippmann and other democratic elite theorists, however, have never been able to discover a successful method for assuring the development of expert *and* politically accountable leaders. "If the self-appointed guardians are capable of protecting the system, is there not a danger that under some circumstances they would be capable of subverting it?"[7] While Lippmann is not sufficiently sensitive to this question, Dewey and others did feel that he had uncovered a real weakness in the democratic armor.

Dewey's objection to Lippmann, as stated in *The Public and Its Problems*, is not that he sees unreal problems, but that he does not see far enough. Dewey, in contrast, inquires into the meaning of the public as an association, not merely as an

7. Bachrach, *The Theory of Democratic Elitism*, p. 54.

aggregation, of individuals. For Dewey, the public means far more than public opinion. It is a concept to define the characteristic features of political activity and the very nature of the state. Lippmann views the public's role as that of an occasional check on governmental power. This, too, can be contrasted with Dewey's picture of the public as participants in a community activity that produces a set of interests represented or looked after by the state.

Dewey begins with a series of specific objections to Lippmann's elitism. In *The Public and Its Problems*, he recognizes, as Lippmann does not, that a government of experts with limited feedback from the masses can never "be anything but an oligarchy managed in the interests of the few." History supports Dewey's judgment that "the world has suffered more from leaders and authorities than from the masses." To Lippmann's criticisms of the quality of public opinion, Dewey makes two points. First, any argument for rule by experts invariably "proves too much for its own cause." That is, if the masses are as irredeemable intellectually as this theory asserts, democracy is impossible. An ignorant public has no way of making its needs and desires known to those at the top; democracy becomes indistinguishable from benevolent despotism. Or the public's uninformed actions will be interpreted as threats to the system by the elite, encouraging them to take undemocratic measures to protect their system. Dewey argues against the assumption that rule by experts will be benevolent or in the common interest. The only way the common interest can be uncovered, he insists, is through the public's participation in governing. Otherwise, experts or not, rulers are "shut off from knowledge of the needs which they are supposed to serve" (pp. 203-9).

Dewey's second argument is the most important. He agrees with Lippmann that the individual by himself is ill equipped with the intelligence necessary for reasonable political action. But in attacking the notion of the "omnicompetent" individual, Lippmann stops short; he does not see that the whole notion rests on a false understanding of the individual. "A single man when he is joined in marriage is different in that connection to what he was as single or to what he is in some other union, as a member, say, of a club. He has new powers and immunities, new responsibilities. He can be contrasted with *himself* as he behaves in other connections. He may be compared and contrasted with his wife in their distinctive roles within the union. But *as* a member of the union he cannot be treated as antithetical to the union, his traits and acts are evidently those which he possesses in virtue of it, while those of the integrated association are what they are in virtue of his status in the union" (p. 189, Dewey's emphasis). As a part of an association, an individual is different from what he is in isolation; the character of an association, on the other hand, is not simply defined by the sum of its members; rather, its nature is determined by the pattern of interaction between individuals. For instance, when we talk about the intelligence of public opinion, the first thing to recognize is that it is the level of *public*, not individual, knowledge and understanding that is important. Intelligence is not merely a "personal endowment or a personal attainment." Knowledge "is a function of association and communication; it depends upon tradition, upon tools and methods socially transmitted, developed and sanctioned" (p. 158). As a member of the public, the individual shares in, and contributes to, the store of social knowledge. Majority rule is never simply majority rule; what is important is the process whereby the majority is formed. Free communication permits men to share their needs and desires and to perceive consequences; the result is a public in fact as well as in name.

    Dewey argues that the main problem of politics is controlling consequences, and he distinguishes immediately two kinds of actions: private and public. Private acts are those in which consequences are confined largely to persons engaged directly in a transaction; for example, activities within the family usually involve only the interests of its members. Man belongs to a variety of groups: church, club, neighborhood gang, professional association. Not all of these groups are political. How a man worships, for example, is a private affair; his activity does not harm others. Worshipping certainly may be a social activity, but it is not public. The larger society's intervention in activities wherein individuals cooperate in some activity without harming others is an "impertinence." But there are other actions whose consequences are so widespread and important as "to need control, whether by inhibition or promotion" (p. 15). These actions are indeed public. "Sometimes the consequences are confined to those who directly share in the transaction which produces them. In other cases they extend far beyond those immediately engaged in producing them. Thus two kinds of interests and of measures of regulation of acts in view of consequences are generated. In the first, interest and control are limited to those directly engaged; in the second, they extend to those who do not directly share in the performance of acts. If, then, the interest constituted by their being affected by the actions in question is to have any practical influence, control over the actions which produce them must occur by some indirect means" (p. 35).

Dewey calls "The Public" those affected indirectly but seriously by the acts of other groups or individuals. The public's interest can be protected or promoted only by an inclusive association that has authority over the entire society. This association is the government: "The public is a political state" (p. 35).

Central to much liberal thought is this belief that drawing a distinction between private and public actions is essential for uncovering the proper limits and uses of the state's power. The issue is seen usually as one of delimiting the respective realms of freedom and authority. Mill, for example, argues a distinction between that part of life "in which it is chiefly the individual who is interested, and the part which chiefly interests society." At a minimum, the acceptance of individual liberty as a value requires that a person be free to do whatever he wants as long as he does not harm the interests of others, even if his actions displease them. Mill is correct to take a stand against the use of legal or social coercions merely because one does not like the actions of another.[8] Nevertheless, as Mill's critics have charged, very few individual actions or interests do not concern society. Mill's distinction between self-regarding

8. Two of the best defenses of the usefulness of Mill's principles are Hart, *Law, Liberty, and Morality*, and J. C. Rees, "A Re-Reading of Mill on Liberty," in Kramnick, *Essays in History of Political Thought*, pp. 357-71. Although I sympathize with both these works, I believe Dewey comes closer to the truth in suggesting that all of men's actions may affect society at some time, and hence be subject to control.

and other-regarding actions cannot provide us with any final criteria for discriminating among those interests which should be left alone and those which society can control.

In contrast to Mill, Dewey eschews any effort to set down some formal principles for drawing the line between private and public acts. Since the consequences of actions change with conditions, the line between private and public shifts constantly; therefore, formal principles are of little use for marking off their respective spheres. By approaching from a very different angle the issue of the distinction between private and public, Dewey consequently escapes many of the objections to Mill's essay. He recognizes that "many private acts are social." For instance, the philanthropist's actions are private but not merely individual: What he does has social consequences. Any exchange between two or more persons is social. The distinction between private and public can be "in no sense equivalent to the distinction between individual and social," even if we grant that this latter distinction has a real meaning, a point which Dewey generally is unwilling to concede (p. 13). The line between private and public must be drawn instead in terms of the different consequences—direct or indirect, narrow or widespread, temporary or irredeemable—of various transactions.

We might expect at this point that Dewey would give us some scheme for classifying consequences in order to distinguish more fully between private and public acts. However, he shifts the issue to the *process* whereby acts are critically evaluated. "Our hypothesis is neutral as to any general, sweeping implications as to how far state activity may extend. It does not indicate any particular policy of public action. . . . The consequences vary with concrete conditions; hence at one time and place a large measure of state activity may be indicated and at another time a policy of quiescence and *laissez-faire.* Just as publics and states vary with conditions of time and place, so do the concrete functions which should be carried on by states. There is no antecedent universal proposition which can be laid down because of which the functions of a state should be limited or should be expanded. Their scope is something to be critically and experimentally determined" (pp. 73-74).

Is Dewey's substitution of a "method" for a set of formal

principles just another example of what his critics would call
an evasion of social, economic, and political problems? In part,
the answer must be yes. That is, it is possible to construct an
argument for associative freedom that satisfies the pragmatist's
demand for flexibility and also provides guidelines for determining whether acts are private or public in Dewey's sense.
Such an argument might be built on the case for treating
impartially men's interests and concerns. For instance, despite
the difficulties with Mill's attempt to draw the line between
private and public acts, his theory does offer a persuasive set of
reasons for leaving individuals alone. The onus of proof is
shifted to those who would regulate the freedom of either the
individual or an association. Or a case for associative freedom
could follow the lines suggested by de Tocqueville. In this view,
voluntary associations are important counterweights to the
state's authority. Of course, none of these discussions will
settle what should be done in a particular case. Formal principles are only guides to conduct; the appropriate conduct will
have to include information about the actual situation. However, one of the reasons pragmatists have so many critics is
because they argue that any discussion of such general principles is a waste of time.

However, it would be a mistake to take at face value Dewey's
criticisms of formal principles. We have been insisting throughout that Dewey's appeal to "method" or "procedure" is the
functional equivalent of a formal philosophy. While that appeal
is open to criticism, Dewey's discussion of the process whereby
the public is formed *contains* principles for distinguishing
between desirable and undesirable state actions. His exploration of how the public is formed is guided by his desire to
uncover a relationship between the individual or associations
and the larger society that will both protect individuality and
define justifiable social control.

In *The Public and Its Problems*, Dewey argues that only
democracy provides a considerable guarantee that the line
between private and public acts will be drawn fairly. The
significance of political democracy, he argues, is that it attempts to arrange political institutions in order to secure
representation of the public interest without violating individual or associative freedom. As a form of government, democ-

racy establishes conditions for discovering freely the "consequences" of actions. The popular election of officials, the principle of majority rule, the freedoms of speech and assembly all make possible an "experimental" and open determination of men's interests. But democracy, Dewey insists, is not just a form of government. If the form is to be matched by substance, democratic government requires an active *demos*—the public. The representatives of the public interest cannot represent that interest if there is no public worthy of the name.

In its richest meaning, community is always a matter of local, face-to-face relationships. A pattern of local community units provides individuals with an important medium through which their interests and individual judgments—expanded and reinforced by participation in the cumulative intelligence of the group—can be represented to the government. This conception of the public gives "a criterion for determining how good a particular state is: namely, the degree of organization of the public which is attained, and the degree in which its officers are so constituted as to perform their function of caring for public interests." Since democracy means the public interest is dominant, Dewey links democracy to community. "Regarded as an idea, democracy is not an alternative to other principles of associated life. It is the idea of community life itself" (pp. 33, 148, 211–13). Democracy and community must blend in turn with communication and free inquiry "if the Great Society is to become a Great Community; a society in which the ever-expanding and intricately ramifying consequences of associated activities shall be known in the full sense of that word, so that an organized, articulate Public comes into being. The highest and most difficult kind of inquiry and a subtle, delicate, vivid and responsive art of communication must take possession of the physical machinery of transmission and circulation and breathe life into it. . . . Democracy will come into its own, for democracy is a name for a life of free and enriching communion. . . . It will have its consummation when free social inquiry is indissolubly wedded to the art of full and moving communication" (p. 184).

The argument that men must participate in, not simply experience, the events which affect them gives Dewey a tool for diagnosing the problems of modern democracy. In the corporate age, impersonal and mechanical relationships have replaced more natural ones. Although modern society has emancipated many persons from old habits, rigid customs, and restrictive institutions, no new pattern of meaningful social connections has arisen to take their place. "The local face-to-face community has been invaded by forces so vast, so remote in initiation, so far-reaching in scope and so complexly indirect in operation, that they are, from the standpoint of the members of local social units, unknown. Man, as has often been remarked, has difficulty in getting on either with or without his fellows, even in neighborhoods. He is not more successful in getting on with them when they act at a great distance in ways invisible to him. An inchoate public is capable of organization only when indirect consequences are perceived, and when it is possible to project agencies which order their occurrence. At present, many consequences are felt rather than perceived; they are suffered, but they cannot be said to be known, for they are not, by those who experience them, referred to their origins. It goes, then, without saying that agencies are not established which canalize the streams of social action and thereby regulate them. Hence the publics are amorphous and unarticulated" (p. 131).

Man's opinions and behavior have become regimented; public opinion is poorly formed and hence mediocre. When associative ties disappear, authority and power become remote. Politics becomes dominated by "bosses with their political machine [who] fill the void between government and the public." Dewey agrees with Lippmann that under such conditions, the public simply "obscures, confuses, and misleads governmental action in a disastrous way" (pp. 120, 125). In the language of participatory democracy, Dewey's position is that although the public may check political power, there is little if any popular political rule. Thus, the democratic experience is parsimonious rather than enriching, restrictive rather than educative, dominated by selfish claims rather than responsive to common interests. Dewey's theory of the democratic public is committed to no particular end. The *style* of politics is the *substance* of politics. It opens up the means whereby men can become committed. It is a theory wherein action defines the ends as well as the means of political life. The nature of the public interest is inseparable from the ways the public is formed. "The essential need, in other words, is the improvement of the methods and conditions of debate, discussion and persuasion. That is *the* problem of the public" (p. 208, Dewey's emphasis).

Under favorable conditions, the formation of the public proceeds through three stages: consequences, perception, and organized action. Certain actions of men in association have large-scale ramifications. If men are not isolated from each other, they become aware of these consequences through communication and through their participation in politics or in the public business. Political purposes, plans, and policies arise as guides to political action: politics is the art of collective problem solving.

This description of political activity probably is too schematic in suggesting a linear progression from one stage to the next. It can be argued that existing political institutions often assume the lead in identifying—or in obscuring—the public interest. But Dewey is painting with broad strokes here to capture the general rhythm of political activity. The direction of a society's politics is determined by the interaction between emerging public needs and wants on the one hand, and institutionalized political forms and machinery on the other. Society is always in a state of flux; the formation of the public thus entails the pressing of new claims, the reconstruction of old interests, and the awareness of new interests. Established institutions, however, tend toward stasis and often are most sensitive to familiar and past claims. Thus, "to form itself, the public has to break existing political forms" (p. 31).

The responsiveness of the state is not something accomplished automatically. Rather, it is something to be attained through continuous political action, through pressure from the community on the state. Since community demands a "concern on the part of each in the joint action and in the contribution of each of its members to it," community is critical to a genuinely democratic experience which makes each man's individuality secure (p. 188). Thus, both collective action and individual liberty are essential for realizing the liberal value of individuality. The existence of a public is a way of resolving the dialectic of social control and individual liberty. Conjoint activity, communication—in a word, community—is as important to the development of personality as the right to be left alone. Throughout *The Public and Its Problems*, Dewey suggests a line of political action and social development which permits the personality of each person to develop in harmony with that of every other person. By placing the idea of community underneath the theory of democracy, Dewey points the direction which must be taken if the values of individual choice and collective social action are to be realized jointly. Our most serious political choices are not between control and individual spontaneity, authority and freedom, the individual good and the common good. Rather we must choose between public policies and political actions which enhance each individual's life and those which enrich only a few.

Dewey gives us a promising beginning for reconstructing much of democratic theory. And although he never discusses explicitly the problem of political obligation, it is not difficult now to find his answer to why men should obey the state. First, Dewey agrees with Lippmann that little is gained from looking at the state in terms of its "authorship." Explanations of the state which refer to the essential nature of man or to some form of a social contract suffer from a common error: "the taking of causal agency instead of consequences as the heart of the problem." Such theories are simply arbitrary formulations: One is as good as another. The major fault of theories which explain the state in terms of "doers of deeds" or authorship is that they foster the false issue of command and obedience. If the state has to be regarded as the product of some will, it "is conceived either as sheer oppression born of arbitrary power and sustained in fraud, or as a pooling of the forces of single men into a massive force which single persons are unable to resist." In short, the state must be explained either in terms of the superior strength of the rulers or as the result of a mythical social contract. The alternative to these theories, Dewey argues, "is surrender of the causal authorship theory and the adoption of that of widely distributed consequences, which, when they are perceived, create a common interest and the need of special agencies to care for it" (pp. 17-22, 54).

Implicit in such statements is the viewpoint that *participation in the creation of the public interest is the basis of political obligation*. The same point is evident in Dewey's identification of democracy with community. Obligation results from the cooperation necessary for collective problem solving. "Where-ever there is conjoint activity," Dewey writes, "whose conse-quences are appreciated as good by all singular persons who take part in it, and where the realization of the good is such as to effect an energetic desire and effort to sustain it in being just because it is a good shared by all, there is in so far a com-munity." Dewey's suggestion that political participation is a sufficient basis for political obligation presumes an ideal set of circumstances. But, as Dewey's own analysis of the public's problem makes clear, the political and moral context within which obligations might occur has been drastically altered in modern societies. Men now live in a corporate society where large, hierarchical institutions pervade their social, economic, and political experiences. Transactions between individuals and institutions are lopsided. The individual, lacking the in-formation and resources available to corporate actors, is often reduced to a spectator unable to understand or influence events. Dewey is not insensitive to such complaints. His solution at times is to emphasize participation in smaller, more intimate groups that bind individuals together. This is the strategy of pluralism which imagines local communities mediating be-tween the individual and larger, more impersonal institutions. But at other times Dewey encourages us to believe that it is possible to form a more inclusive public that unites the interests of local groups. What he does not sufficiently appreciate is that participation in smaller groups—with the obligations that cre-ates—might well preclude cooperation with more inclusive bodies. Participation—the source of obligation—in different associations may well lead to competing rather than reinforcing obligations.

When publics conflict or when the will of the individual clashes with the will of the larger group, one can understand Bertrand Russell's complaint that Dewey's philosophy is a power philosophy which values the power of the community or state rather than that of the individual.[9] Russell's warning takes on added significance when we examine what Dewey says about law.

Since the state is the organization of the public to control the

9. *Public and Its Problems*, p. 149; Russell, *History of Western Philosophy*, p. 827.

consequences of men's actions, Dewey contends that law is misunderstood when regarded as a series of commands. Such a view of law, he argues, leads one to look for the will behind the commands. Men become preoccupied with such questions as why the rulers should have authority, why men should submit to the law. Such questions disappear, however, once we recognize that "rules of laws are in fact the institution of conditions under which persons make their arrangements with one another" (*Public and Its Problems*, p. 54). Relying on the language of consequences, Dewey makes law the very embodiment of the good sense of the community. "What happens is that certain conditions are set such that *if* a person conforms to them, he can count on certain consequences, while if he fails to do so he cannot forecast consequences. . . . There is no reason to interpret even the 'prohibitions' of criminal law in any other way. Conditions are stated in reference to consequences which may be incurred if they are infringed or transgressed. . . . 'The law' formulates remote and long-run consequences. It then operates as a condensed available check on the naturally overweening influence of immediate desire and interest over decision. It is a means of doing for a person what otherwise only his own foresight, if thoroughly reasonable, could do. . . . Upon this theory, the law as 'embodied reason' means a formulated generalization of means and procedures in behavior which are adapted to secure what is wanted" (pp. 55-57, Dewey's emphasis).

In the foregoing, Dewey locates the rationality of political authority in the collective act of intelligence. Since law accomplishes what the individual acting alone cannot—and since instrumentalism measures acts by their consequences—Dewey regards positive law as both reasonable and natural. This viewpoint makes it difficult to imagine grounds upon which one could challenge the law. It also obscures the fact that laws often favor some persons at the expense of others. Again, Dewey erases conflict from his account of politics. Political power is viewed merely as an instrument, used well or poorly, to desired ends. Of itself, it requires no searching examination. Thus, Dewey takes for granted that when conditions exist for creating a public, there also exists a sufficient basis for political action and, hence, for obligation. This view rests on Dewey's account of how problems arise and on his faith that creative intelligence can resolve most, if not all, social conflicts. Insofar as these arguments are cast in doubt, we cannot be satisfied with his answer to why a man is obliged to obey the state.

DEMOCRACY AS A WAY OF LIFE

Dewey is both a theorist of democracy and a democratic theorist; that is, his theory of democracy is intertwined with his philosophy of the democratic possibilities of a wide range of experiences, from the art of thinking to the art of planning, from what takes place in the school to what occurs in the factory. The result is a theory of technique or method on the one hand, and a doctrine of desirable ends on the other. Democracy carries a heavy load of meanings in Dewey's work. It is a form of government, a set of procedures and freedoms for making the state responsible to the public, and a way of life, one marked by the spread of the "intelligent" or "scientific" attitude within all social institutions.

Although the two cannot be separated in the end, Dewey advances both an empirical and a normative set of reasons for viewing democracy as more than a form of government. Within the descriptive framework of social realities as culture and human nature as interactions, political institutions and political behavior are viewed as parts of a larger web of relationships. For example, while political and legal institutions shape other associations in society, they obviously are affected by those associations. One cannot portray accurately the operations or the significance of a particular dimension of society without referring to the larger context of which it is a part. In *Freedom and Culture*, Dewey contends that the fault with most theories of democracy is that they regard as the whole only one part of the interaction between the individual and cultural conditions, or between the political and other aspects of society. Most democratic theorists begin with the individual as a given; this failure to see the individual in relationship to his environment leads them to mistake the problem of democracy as essentially a personal one. To be sure, early democratic theorists were aware of the relationships between economics and politics, for example. But they thought that self-government could be assured simply by establishing certain procedures for making officials accountable to the people. They assumed that every individual desires freedom, and that control of representatives exhausts the requirements for self-government.

Once the interdependency of man's nature and all aspects of a culture is recognized, it becomes clear that human nature does not necessarily dictate democratic institutions. Everything Dewey says about the forces of economic combination, the breakdown of community life, and the increasing significance of impersonal forces in controlling the course of events supports his conclusion that the very idea of democracy is now subject to basic strain. The lesson to be learned is that "the struggle for democracy has to be maintained on as many fronts as culture has aspects: political, economic, international, educational, scientific and artistic, religious" (*Freedom and Culture*, pp. 57–61, 173).

The basis of democracy is "faith in the capacities of human nature; faith in human intelligence and in the power of pooled and cooperative experience." Although intelligence is distributed unequally, the democrat affirms that each individual has something vital to contribute, and that the process of experience is itself educative. Dewey values democracy as the setting within which the experimental method of thought and action can take place. This is not simply a commitment to method; it is a commitment to the worth of each individual. For instance, political democracy is important because it removes many of the restrictions that prevent the individual from having a share in shaping and directing the social institutions which affect him. Political democracy affirms that each person "is equally an individual and entitled to equal opportunity in development of his own capacities, be they large or small in range."[10] Dewey values political democracy as a way to check some abuses of power. But since a major goal of democracy is growth in the capacities of each individual, positive conditions are needed also. In a crucial essay, "Democracy and Educational Administration," he writes that "the political and governmental phase

10. Dewey, "Democracy and Educational Administration," in *Problems of Men*, p. 60.

of democracy is a means, the best means so far found for realizing ends that lie in the wide domain of human relationships and the development of human personality. It is, as we often say, though perhaps without appreciating all that is involved in the saying, a way of life, social and individual. The keynote of democracy as a way of life may be expressed, it seems to me, as the necessity for the participation of every mature human being in formation of the values that regulate the living of men together: which is necessary from the standpoint of both the general social welfare and the full development of humans beings as individuals" (pp. 57-58).

The commitment to intelligence in Dewey's theory of democracy is a commitment to *participation* and to *ideas in action*. On participation, Dewey argues: "Personality must be educated, and personality cannot be educated by confining its operations to technical and specialized things, or to the less important relationships of life. Full education comes only when there is a responsible share on the part of each person, in proportion to capacity, in shaping the aims and policies of the social groups to which he belongs. This fact fixes the significance of democracy." But education to the idea, to the meaning, of democracy is not sufficient. As the needs of men change and new ones arise, the political, economic, and social institutions must be responsive in providing "new resources for satisfying those needs." This can be accomplished only when the democratic idea is "constantly discovered, and rediscovered, remade and reorganized."[11] Democracy as a way of life affirms the values of individuality and community both as means and as ends. The characteristic features of instrumentalism—inquiry, communication, experimental action—point also to the end: the growth of individual personality through participation and cooperation with others in controlling social forces and in making associations purposeful. The state is only one among many form of associations, but it has a very special purpose—to safeguard common interests. Again, the end is also the means: The state can function properly only to the extent it respects the community as a source of legitimate claims. Dewey does not assume, although he is confident, that what men want will

11. Dewey, *Reconstruction*, p. 209; "Challenge of Democracy to Education," in *Problems of Men*, p. 47.

always be congruent with what needs to be done to solve the problems of men. His hopes for democracy pivot on the belief that in a genuine community, men's wants and their needs will come together. There are no guarantees; but "a free man," Dewey writes, "would rather take his chance in an open world than be guaranteed in a closed world" (*Human Nature and Conduct*, p. 285).

7. The Retrieval of Liberalism

DEWEY'S CONCERN with testing ideas *through* action often gets in the way of his effort to provide us with a clear guide *to* action. In part, he poses a false dilemma for political theory. Arguing that concrete problems demand specific cures, he wrongly concludes that our ideas must also be narrowed down to specific hypotheses. If by problem solving we mean only that type of action engaged in by men as they actually make particular decisions or choices, then it is clear that formal principles and broad theories cannot "solve" problems. But rational and moral problem solving requires also that we stand back from the immediate pressures of technical decision making or, to change the imagery but not the meaning, from the demands of the movement. Both pragmatists and incrementalists argue that the conditions and circumstances within which a particular decision is reached determine its appropriateness. Both are correct in arguing that the exigencies of the moment may justify overriding a priori rules or principles. But if political actions and decisions are to be moral, we need to know when we are making exceptions to the principled type of rules set down by morality with its insistence on consistency, similarity, and

122

impartiality.[1] Dewey's emphasis on trial-and-error, the here-and-now, is not sufficiently sensitive to this issue. On closer inspection, his pragmatism avoids overriding moral directives; but it is difficult, rather than easy, to see the moral rules implicit in his appeals to method.

Nevertheless, Dewey's insistence that action and its consequences are critical to any valid theory of politics is important. A positive philosophy for improving social life will not be discovered unless we learn to test our concepts, theories, and judgments in terms which ultimately refer to the experiences of concrete individuals. All too frequently, political theory has committed many of the sins for which Dewey criticizes it. The manipulation of concepts and an endless parade of "the newest approach" to the study of man and society, characteristic of political science, are of little avail if they resolve the imaginary problems of imaginary men. Pitfalls do surround the demand for knowledge which is relevant or socially useful, particularly the temptation to substitute appealing slogans for rigorous thought.[2] But Dewey's work demonstrates that the alternative to formalism need not be mere rhetoric. His writings have captured the attention of a large audience, precisely because he relates his concern with the problems of men to an analysis of the methods of inquiry needed to solve those problems. Unless one believes with Pangloss that the world is the best of all possible worlds, there will always be a need for men to cast off "intellectual timidity" and to ask what sort of action the "facts" exact of us.

Dewey's tough-minded insistence on solving specific problems is part of his vision of a democratically organized community. This corresponds to his conception of the dual function of philosophy as the logic of method and the art of criticism. Generally, he is more successful in bringing together his method and his vision than many of his critics allow. Indeed, he is often

1. See Schoettle, Letter to the Editor, and Frohock, *Normative Political Theory*, pp. 102–5.
2. David Kettler reminds us that there is "an urgent need to rehabilitate the theoretical enterprise . . . to reinstate distinctions between slogans for mobilization and analyses for orientation, between polemical annihilation and mutual criticism, between ideas as political instruments alone and theory." Kettler's own essay is an important contribution to this task of rehabilitation ("Vocation of Radical Intellectuals," p. 26).

at his best when describing the positive roles for political philosophy. Once men address problems, select and eliminate "facts," and form laws or principles for interpreting the facts, they begin to suggest things to do and not to do, they begin to change men's attitudes toward the world. Dewey's admiration for the scientific mode of analysis never deteriorates into that sort of scientific mood which ignores value judgments. "Anything that obscures the fundamentally moral nature of the social problem is harmful. . . . Any doctrine that eliminates or even obscures the function of choice of values and enlistment of desires and emotions in behalf of those chosen weakens personal responsibility for judgment and for action" (*Freedom and Culture*, p. 172).

Dewey's more specific contributions to political theory are also considerable. But among them, two stand out: his comprehension of man as a communal being and his defense of democracy. Dewey makes more secure liberalism's two most important values—individuality and freedom of inquiry—by tying both to the experience of community and the art of communication.

Liberalism currently has more critics than defenders. Traditional liberalism's understanding of man and its defense of democracy as an arena for pursuing particularistic interests have been especially vulnerable to criticism. To argue for a wide range of free choices and actions on the basis that there exists an area of behavior which concerns merely the individual commits the liberal to the almost impossible task of distinguishing the individual and the social. And there is a widespread feeling that even if the liberal teaching could be practiced, it entails a very low standard of good human relations— mutual forebearance at best, mutual indifference at worst.[3]

Liberals have been often suspicious of the idea of community; fraternity always tends to be slighted in favor of liberty and equality. This suspicion is evident in John Stuart Mill's warning "that so few now dare to be eccentric marks the chief danger

3. In this part of my summary of Dewey's contributions I am indebted greatly to Glenn Tinder's effort to place the ideal of tolerance on stronger grounds by separating it from individualist assumptions and by grounding it in the notion of community. Unfortunately, Tinder's work (*Tolerance*) appeared too late to be used to test my own ideas.

of our time."[4] Classical liberalism's defense of the individual's right to do and to think as he pleases still has a common-sense appeal. We do want protection from those who would use techniques of coercion and manipulation to create community and like-mindedness. But at the same time, people do care for each other. Man's desire for unity is as much a part of his nature as is his need for autonomy. By outlining the close relationship between community and communication, Dewey forges a new alliance between the liberal value of free choice and action on the one side and fraternity on the other. Thus, he retrieves liberalism from both the traditional liberal and the current critics of liberalism's excessive individualism.

Dewey's theory that the individual's identity is a social identity seems most in keeping with what we know about the role of social forces in shaping a person's life. Man succumbs often to social forces in ways which he does not even comprehend. Man is never autonomous—if that means his choices and actions are never dependent on, or influenced by, his environment. Dewey formulates the problem of man's relationship to society in terms very similar to Rousseau. The problem, Rousseau writes, is "'how to find a form of association which will defend the person and goods of each member with the collective force of all, and under which each individual, while uniting himself with the others, obeys no one but himself, and remains as free as before.'"[5] Man cannot escape from society; Dewey, in a fashion more liberal than Rousseau, understands the nature of that community which secures the common among men without overriding the differences. For Dewey, community is not a closed, habitual association. Unity does not mean uniformity. Because traditional liberalism values individualism, it concludes that autonomy and community are hostile ideas. This hostility equates community and uniformity. But community, Dewey insists strongly, does not mean an all-embracing uniformity: It means communication. Man retains his individuality within the community as long as he is free to communicate. Tolerance, inquiry, and communication enable individuals to live well by learning through doing. In this fashion, practice leads to growth in individual personality and

4. *Utilitarianism, Liberty, and Representative Government*, p. 167.
5. Rousseau, *Social Contract*, p. 60.

in interpersonal relationships. Communication affirms individuality and community.

Dewey's defense of democracy telescopes the meanings of community and democracy. In numerous ways, he attempts to recover man's capacity to be a part of a self-determining society. The individualism of earlier liberalism views politics as important mainly as a guarantee of man's ability to pursue utilitarian gratifications. The individuality of Dewey's renascent liberalism understands politics as the arena where men discover collective goals and undertake common enterprises to promote the freedom of the whole.

The widespread view that liberalism reduces political activity to the self-interested behavior characteristic of the free market economy ignores the thread of community within the liberal thought of such writers as Dewey.[6] There are numerous difficulties with Dewey's attempt to reconcile liberal values and communitarian themes, but he was aware of the interdependence between the two. He wanted a society where each individual could develop his tastes and talents free from senseless restrictions. Too often, he argued, personality is cramped within narrow boundaries which are either outdated or immoral. The organization of the school, the structure of the work place, and the operations of the political system often encourage uniformity and complacency. Thus, Dewey constantly fought to abolish the rigid routines and authoritarian teaching methods which make the classroom a joyless and oppressive place. He criticized an economic system possessing the means but not the will to free men from economic insecurity, and, more important, for failing to provide men with room to exercise their independence, vigor, and initiative. In politics, Dewey valued fraternity because he saw in the principle of cooperation and communication the only sure way to individuality. Liberty is a personal enjoyment that has to be achieved collectively.

While Dewey emphasized the special role of the school in evoking and transmitting the sentiments and skills needed in a democratic community, he did not limit the idea of education to schooling. Rather, the entire culture and organization of society must be judged in terms of its educative impact on man's

6. For a solid argument against Hartz's monolithic portrayal of the liberal tradition in America, for example, see Price, "Community and Control."

character. Education is the tool for improving society, and a democratic education establishes the goals for society. The task of education and political thought, Dewey argued, is to make sense of the environment surrounding a man, to relate events which occur on the external scene to the inner life of man and to his fortunes and misfortunes. Philosophy's purpose is to supply the individual with an orientation which makes sense of current troubles and difficulties by explaining the interactions between man and society. This, Dewey believed, is the only way "in which the philosopher can look his fellow man in the face with frankness and with humanity." This is still a worthwhile aspiration for political philosophy.

Bibliography

A valuable guide to John Dewey's works and to works about him is the bibliography compiled by Milton Halsey Thomas, *John Dewey: A Centennial Bibliography*. Chicago: University of Chicago Press, 1962.

DEWEY'S WORKS CITED

Dewey, John. *Characters and Events: Popular Essays in Social and Political Philosophy*. Edited by Joseph Ratner. 2 vols. New York: Henry Holt & Co., 1929.
———. *Democracy and Education: An Introduction to the Philosophy of Education*. 1916. Reprint. New York: Macmillan Co., Free Press, 1966.
———. *Essays in Experimental Logic*. 1916. Reprint. New York: Dover Publications, 1953.
———, and Tufts, James H. *Ethics*. New York: Henry Holt & Co., 1908.
———. *The Ethics of Democracy*. University of Michigan Philosophical Papers, 2d series, no. 1. Ann Arbor: Andrews & Co., 1888.
———. *Experience and Education*. 1938. Reprint. New York: Macmillan Co., Collier Books, 1963.
———. *Freedom and Culture*. 1939. Reprint. New York: G. P. Putnam's Sons, Capricorn Books, 1963.
———. "The Future of Radical Political Action." *Nation*, 4 January 1933, pp. 8-9.
———. *Human Nature and Conduct: An Introduction to Social Psychology*. 1922. Reprint. New York: Random House, Modern Library, 1930.
———. *Individualism Old and New*. 1930. Reprint. New York: G. P. Putnam's Sons, Capricorn Books, 1962.

——. *The Influence of Darwin on Philosophy: And Other Essays in Contemporary Thought.* 1910. Reprint. New York: Peter Smith, 1951.

——. *Intelligence in the Modern World: John Dewey's Philosophy.* Edited by Joseph Ratner. New York: Random House, Modern Library, 1939.

——, and Bentley, Arthur F. *Knowing and the Known.* Boston: Beacon Press, 1949.

——. *Liberalism and Social Action.* 1935. Reprint. New York: G. P. Putnam's Sons, Capricorn Books, 1963.

——. "The Need for Social Psychology." *Psychological Review* 24 (1917):266-77.

——. *On Experience, Nature, and Freedom: Representative Selections.* Edited by Richard J. Bernstein. Indianapolis, Ind.: Bobbs-Merrill Co., Liberal Arts Press, 1960.

——. *Outlines of a Critical Theory of Ethics.* 1891. Reprint. New York: Hillary House, 1957.

——. *Problems of Men.* New York: Philosophical Library, 1946.

——. *The Public and Its Problems.* 1927. Reprint. Chicago: Swallow Press, Sage Books, [n.d.].

——. *The Quest for Certainty: A Study of the Relation of Knowledge and Action.* 1929. Reprint. New York: G. P. Putnam's Sons, Capricorn Books, 1960.

——. *Reconstruction in Philosophy.* 1920. Reprint. Boston: Beacon Press, 1957.

——. *The School and Society.* Chicago: University of Chicago Press, 1900.

——. *Studies in Logical Theory.* Chicago: University of Chicago Press, 1903.

——. *Theory of Valuation.* International Encyclopedia of Unified Science, vol. 2, no. 4. Chicago: University of Chicago Press, 1939.

——. "Why I Am Not a Communist." *Modern Monthly,* April 1934, pp. 135-37.

OTHER WORKS CITED

Adler, Mortimer J. *The Idea of Freedom: A Dialectical Examination of the Conceptions of Freedom.* 2 vols. Garden City, N. Y.: Doubleday & Co., 1958, 1961.

Bachrach, Peter. *The Theory of Democratic Elitism: A Critique.* Boston: Little, Brown & Co., 1967.

Benn, S. I., and Peters, R. S. *The Principles of Political Thought.* New York: Macmillan Co., Free Press, 1965.

Berleson, Bernard, et al. *Voting.* Chicago: University of Chicago Press, 1954.

Berlin, Isaiah. *Four Essays on Liberty.* New York: Oxford University Press, 1969.

Bernstein, Richard J. *Praxis and Action: Contemporary Philosophies of Human Activity.* Philadelphia: University of Pennsylvania Press, 1971.

Bourne, Randolph S. *War and the Intellectuals.* Edited by Carl Resek. New York: Harper & Row, 1964.

Cohen, Morris. *Studies in Philosophy and Science.* New York: Frederick Ungar Publishing Co., 1949.

Coleman, James S. *Power and the Structure of Society.* New York: W. W. Norton & Co., 1974.

Connolly, William, ed. *The Bias of Pluralism.* New York: Atherton Press, 1969.

Cook, Samuel. "An Inquiry into the Ethical Foundations of Democracy." Ph.D. dissertation, Ohio State University, 1954.

Cranston, Maurice. *Freedom*. 3d ed., rev. New York: Basic Books, 1967.

Crick, Bernard. *In Defence of Politics*. Rev. ed. Baltimore: Penguin Books, 1964.

Damico, Alfonso J. "Analysis and Advocacy: Pragmatism and the Study of Politics." *Polity* 7 (1974):193–208.

Dye, Thomas R., and Zeigler, Harmon L. *The Irony of Democracy*. North Scituate, Mass.: Duxbury Press, 1975.

Elliott, William Yandell. *The Pragmatic Revolt in Politics: Syndicalism, Fascism, and the Constitutional State*. New York: Macmillan Co., 1928.

Flacks, Richard. "On the Uses of Participatory Democracy." *Dissent* 13 (1966): 701–8.

Forcey, Charles. *The Crossroads of Liberalism: Croly, Weyl, Lippmann, and the Progressive Era (1900–1925)*. New York: Oxford University Press, 1967.

Fosdick, Dorothy. *What Is Liberty?* New York: Harper & Bros., 1939.

Frankfort, Henry, et al. *Before Philosophy: The Intellectual Adventure of Ancient Man*. 1946. Reprint. Baltimore: Penguin Books, 1961.

Frohock, Fred M. *Normative Political Theory*. Englewood Cliffs, N.J.: Prentice-Hall, 1974.

Green, T. H. *Lectures on the Principles of Political Obligation*. Ann Arbor: University of Michigan Press, 1967.

Halévy, Elie. *The Growth of Philosophic Radicalism*. Boston: Beacon Press, 1960.

Hart, H. L. A. *Law, Liberty, and Morality*. New York: Random House, Vintage Books, 1963.

Hartz, Louis. *The Liberal Tradition in America: An Interpretation of American Political Thought since the Revolution*. New York: Harcourt, Brace & World, Harvest Books, 1955.

Hayek, Friedrich, *The Road to Serfdom*. Chicago: University of Chicago Press, Phoenix Books, 1963.

Hobhouse, Leonard T. *Liberalism*. New York: Oxford University Press, Galaxy Books, 1964.

Hofstadter, Richard. *Anti-Intellectualism in American Life*. New York: Random House, Vintage Books, 1963.

Hook, Sidney. *John Dewey: An Intellectual Portrait*. New York: John Day Co., 1939.

Hullfish, H. Gordon. *Toward a Democratic Education*. Institute for Democratic Education. Columbus: Ohio State University College of Education, 1960.

James, William. *Collected Essays and Reviews*. New York: Longmans, Green & Co., 1920.

———. *The Will to Believe: And Other Essays in Popular Philosophy*. New York: Longmans, Green & Co., 1897.

Kaplan, Abraham. *The Conduct of Inquiry: Methodology for Behavioral Science*. San Francisco: Chandler Publishing Co., 1964.

Kaufman, Arnold S. *The Radical Liberal: The New Politics, Theory and Practice*. New York: Simon and Schuster, Clarion Books, 1970.

Kettler, David. "The Vocation of Radical Intellectuals." *Politics and Society* 1 (1970):23–49.

Keynes, Edward, and Ricci, David M., eds. *Political Power, Community and Democracy*. Chicago: Rand McNally, 1970.

King, Preston, and Parekh, Bhikhu, eds. *Politics and Experience: Essays Presented to Professor Michael Oakeshott on the Occasion of His Retirement*. London: Cambridge University Press, 1968.

Kramnick, Isaac, ed. *Essays in the History of Political Thought*. Englewood Cliffs, N. J.: Prentice-Hall, 1969.

Kuhn, Thomas S. *The Structure of Scientific Revolutions*. Chicago: University of Chicago Press, Phoenix Books, 1964.

Lasch, Christopher. *The New Radicalism in America (1889-1963): The Intellectual as a Social Type*. New York: Random House, Vintage Books, 1967.

Lindblom, Charles. *The Intelligence of Democracy: Decision Making through Mutual Adjustment*. New York: Macmillan Co., Free Press, 1965.

Lippmann, Walter. *The Phantom Public*. New York: Harcourt, Brace & Co., 1925.

———. *Public Opinion*. New York: Macmillan Co., Free Press, 1965.

Macpherson, C. B. *Democratic Theory: Essays in Retrieval*. Oxford: Clarendon Press, 1973.

McDonald, Lee Cameron. *Western Political Theory: From Its Origins to the Present*. New York: Harcourt, Brace & World, 1968.

Marx, Karl, "Critique of the Gotha Program." In *The Marx-Engels Reader*, edited by Robert C. Tucker. New York: W. W. Norton & Co., 1972.

Mill, John Stuart. *Utilitarianism, Liberty, and Representative Government*. New York: E. P. Dutton & Co., Everyman's Library, 1951.

Mills, C. Wright. *Sociology and Pragmatism: The Higher Learning in America*. Edited by Irving Louis Horowitz. New York: Oxford University Press, Galaxy Books, 1966.

———. *The Sociological Imagination*. New York: Grove Press, 1961.

Minar, David W., and Greer, Scott, eds. *The Concept of Community*. Chicago: Aldine Publishing Co., 1969.

Moore, Edward C. *American Pragmatism: Peirce, James, and Dewey*. New York: Columbia University Press, 1961.

Nathanson, Jerome. *John Dewey: The Reconstruction of the Democratic Life*. New York: Charles Scribner's Sons, 1951.

Oppenheim, Felix. "Relativism, Absolutism, and Democracy." *The American Political Science Review* 54 (1950):951-60.

Pateman, Carol. *Participation and Democratic Theory*. Cambridge: Cambridge University Press, 1970.

Peirce, Charles Sanders. *Collected Papers of Charles Sanders Peirce*. 8 vols. Vols. 1-6 edited by C. Hartshorne and P. Weiss. Vols. 7, 8 edited by A. W. Berks. Cambridge: Harvard University Press, 1931-35; 1958.

Pranger, Robert J. *The Eclipse of Citizenship: Power and Participation in Contemporary Politics*. New York: Holt, Rinehart, & Winston, 1968.

Price, David E. "Community and Control: Critical Democratic Theory in the Progressive Period." *The American Political Science Review* 68 (1974):1663-78.

Ratner, Sidney, ed. *The Philosopher of the Common Man: Essays in Honor of John Dewey to Celebrate His Eightieth Birthday*. New York: G. P. Putnam's Sons, 1940.

Richter, Melvin. *The Politics of Conscience: T. H. Green and His Age*. Cambridge: Harvard University Press, 1964.

Rousseau, Jean-Jacques. *The Social Contract*. Translated by Maurice Cranston. Baltimore: Penguin Books, 1974.

Russell, Bertrand. *A History of Western Philosophy*. New York: Simon and Schuster, Clarion Books, 1967.

Sabine, George H. *A History of Political Theory*. 3d ed. New York: Holt, Rinehart, & Winston, 1961.

———. "The Pragmatic Approach to Political Science." *The American Political Science Review* 24 (1930):865-86.

Sartori, Giovanni. *Democratic Theory*. New York: Frederick A. Praeger, 1965.

Schilpp, Paul Arthur, ed. *The Philosophy of John Dewey*. Library of Living

Philosophers, vol. 1. Evanston and Chicago: Northwestern University Press, 1939.

Schoettle, C. B. Letter to the Editor. *The American Political Science Review* 64 (1970):1268-72.

Schumpeter, Joseph A. *Capitalism, Socialism and Democracy*. 3d ed. New York: Harper & Row, 1962.

Shannon, David A. *The Socialist Party of America: A History*. Chicago: Quadrangle Books, 1967.

Somjee, A. H. *The Political Theory of John Dewey*. New York: Teachers College Press, 1968.

Spitz, David. *Essays in the Liberal Idea of Freedom*. Tucson: University of Arizona Press, 1964.

———. "Politics and the Critical Imagination." *The Review of Politics* 32 (1970): 419-35.

Steibel, Gerald Lee. "John Dewey's Philosophy of Democracy Applied in a Critique of Classical Liberalism." Ph.D. dissertation, Columbia University, 1951.

Tinder, Glenn. *Tolerance: Toward a New Civility*. Amherst: University of Massachusetts Press, 1976.

Walzer, Michael. *Obligations: Essays on Disobedience, War, and Citizenship*. Cambridge: Harvard University Press, 1970.

Welter, Rush. *Popular Education and Democratic Thought in America*. New York: Columbia University Press, 1965.

White, Morton. *Science and Sentiment in America: Philosophical Thought from Jonathan Edwards to John Dewey*. New York: Oxford University Press, 1972.

———. *Social Thought in America: The Revolt against Formalism*. Boston: Beacon Press, 1957.

Wolff, Robert Paul. *The Poverty of Liberalism*. Boston: Beacon Press, 1968.

Wood, Allen W. "The Marxian Critique of Justice." *Philosophy and Public Affairs* 1 (1972):244-82.

Index